Lost Souls: FOUND!™

Inspiring Stories About German Shepherd Dogs

Kyla Duffy and Lowrey Mumford

Published by Happy Tails Books™, LLC

Happy Tails Books™ (HTB) uses the power of storytelling to effect positive changes in the lives of animals in need. The joy, hope, and (occasional) chaos these stories describe will make you laugh and cry, as you em*bark* on a journey with these authors who are guardians and/or fosters of adopted dogs. "Reading for Rescue" with HTB not only brings further awareness to rescue efforts and breed characteristics, but each sale also results in a financial contribution to dog rescue groups.

Lost Souls: Found!™ Inspiring Stories About German Shepherd Dogs by Kyla Duffy and Lowrey Mumford

Published by Happy Tails Books™, LLC   www.happytailsbooks.com

The publisher gratefully acknowledges the numerous German Shepherd Dog rescue groups and their members, who generously granted permission to use their stories and photos.

The following brand names are registered trademarks and the property of their owners. The author and publishing company make no claims to the logos mentioned in this book including: Tigger, Kuranda, Road Runner, Energizer Bunny, La-Z-Boy, Pup-A-Roni, Walmart, Nylabone, Frisbee, Petsmart, Petfinder.com.

Photo Credits (All Rights Reserved by Photographers):

>   Front Cover: *Brujac,* Dave Echols
>   Back Cover Top: *Cocoa,* Chris Wilson
>   Back Cover L: *Shadow,* Chris Wilson
>   Back Cover Mid: *Nicky, Chloe, and Nigel,* Annmarie Mikelski
>   Back Cover R: *Dagwood*, Chris Wilson
>   Inside Title: *Nigel,* Annmarie Mikelski
>   P12: *Merci,* Dave Echols

Publishers Cataloging In Publication

Lost Souls: Found!™ Inspiring Stories About German Shepherd Dogs/ [Compiled and edited by] Kyla Duffy and Lowrey Mumford.

p. ; cm.

ISBN: 978-0-9824895-7-4

1. German Shepherd Dogs. 2. Dog rescue. 3. Dogs – Anecdotes. 4. Animal welfare – United States. 5. Human-animal relationships – Anecdotes. I. Duffy, Kyla. II. Mumford, Lowrey. III. Title.

SF426.5   2010

636.737   2010901920

Happy Tails Books appreciates all of the contributors and rescue groups whose thought-provoking stories make this book come to life. We'd like to send a special thanks to:

Coastal White German Shepherd Rescue
http:/www.coastalwgsdrr.org/

Garden State German Shepherd Rescue
http://www.gsgsr.org/

German Shepherd Dog Rescue Group of GA
http://www.gashepherd.org/

German Shepherd Dog Rescue of Central Alabama
http://www.petfinder.com/shelters/gsdcentral.html

German Shepherd Rescue of Orange County
http://www.gsroc.org/

Greater California German Shepherd Rescue
http://www.gcgsr.org/

Hot Water Rescue
http://www.hotwaterrescue.com/

North Louisiana German Shepherd Rescue
http://members.petfinder.org/~LA152/index.html

Want more info about the dogs, authors, and rescues featured in this book? *http://happytailsbooks.com*

Table of Contents

Introduction: New to Rescue

Thinking back, animals have been a huge part of my life since I was very young, and I've always loved them. My parents bred Huskies and sold the puppies to very nice people. Some of my favorite pictures from my youth are of me in a pile of puppies, with a huge smile across my face. I guess it was inevitable that I would eventually become involved with rescue.

As I grew, I learned that not everyone treated puppies and dogs the same way I did, and it hurt my heart. I would watch television shows like *ASPCA New York* on Animal Planet and get upset to the point of tears because I could not understand how and why people would treat defenseless animals with such cruelty.

I knew I wanted to help, and so the first thing I did was insist that all of my family's dogs from then on out be "pound puppies." Walking around shelters and rescues always made me sad because I wished I could take them all home. Of course, I could not, but knowing I was going to help at least one dog find its way to a nice home always brought a smile to my face. And when I recently moved back home from college with my own pound puppy, Gaz, in tow, I became involved with German Shepherd Rescue of Orange County (GSROC).

I've learned much from Gaz and the other rescue dogs I've met, and one thing I can say for sure is that rescue dogs need time. Animals have personalities just like humans: some are shy, some are happy and bounce like Tigger, some are hardworking, some are courageous, some are destructive, and some get so mad when you leave that they give you a present in your favorite shoes! Though many seem scared at first, after some time in their new homes a different personality usually emerges. For example, Gaz wasn't always open to people, and even to this day, she still gets anxious around strangers. But with patience and time she has become much more loving and less afraid.

From day one working with GSROC, I could see how much these kind people, these volunteers, love what they do. They all know the names of over thirty dogs at a time who revolve through the rescue, and I surprised myself by being able to learn them, too. (Excitement is a great motivator.)

GSROC boards their dogs at kennels or fosters them in people's homes, as they don't have a shelter. On Fridays my boyfriend and I visit one of the kennels to walk and bathe the dogs, and on Saturdays we join the other volunteers at pet stores where GSROC has adoption days. We pick up German Shepherds from shelters and rescues, they come in from their foster homes and boarding kennels, and we do our best to find them perfect forever homes.

All of the volunteers sit with these "lost souls" for hours in the sun or the rain, hoping at least one will be adopted by a nice family. The first adoption event can be nerve-wracking for a new volunteer, but I'll never forget how both the dogs and the experienced volunteers made me feel welcome. Additionally I got to sit with a great dog named Kaleigh, who went from wandering the streets with no tags or collar to getting adopted that day by a great family.

That moment made the rest of my week, and that's what this book is about. These stories, authored by people who have fostered and adopted from different rescues and shelters all over the country, share the wonderful feelings you get from helping animals who can't help themselves. You'll laugh and cry as you read about life with rescued German Shepherd Dogs, and you'll hopefully end up like me, inspired to give your spare time to the dogs instead of just wishing someone else would help them. Enjoy!

Brittany Frembling, GSROC Volunteer

Inspiring Stories About German Shepherd Dogs

"He is your friend, your partner, your defender, your dog. You are his life, his love, his leader.

He will be yours, faithful and true, to the last beat of his heart. You owe it to him to be worthy of such devotion."

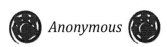 *Anonymous*

17,228 Teaspoons of Peanut Butter

J ane is one of those friends who comes into your life unexpectedly and changes it in ways you never imagined possible.

I was living in Dublin, Ireland, and had just spent the summer training our puppy, Bongo. It was October 1st, my first day of grad school, and Bongo and I were taking an early morning walk when we passed a guy and his annoying dog at a traffic light. I remember thinking, "Man, I'm glad I don't have to deal with that kind of dog."

As we headed for home after walking our lap, we noticed the man was gone, but the dog was still at that traffic light.

She apparently wasn't that guy's dog after all; she was just there on that corner, waiting for a home...so she just followed us. We lived near a busy road, and I didn't want the dog to get hurt, so I put her in the back garden for the day while I went off to school. We named her Jane, for "Jane Doe," and assumed we'd have her for a few days, find her owner, and that would be it. That was nearly 12 years and more than 17,000 teaspoons of peanut butter ago.

Jane quickly made herself part of the pack and established herself as Bongo's sister, protector, and buddy. They went everywhere with us and were quite the Irish duo: Black (Jane) and Tan (Bongo).

Upon moving back to the States, Jane took to Boulder, Colorado, like most of us transplants do, loving the sun and exercise opportunities. I have no idea how that poor dog was born in Ireland because in Colorado she would sit on a hot deck, basking in the 90+ degree heat, panting away, happy as can be. We even made a perch for her at the fireplace, where she would sit against the glass until her hair singed. She couldn't get enough of the warmth!

Jane's time on the streets gave her amazing survival instincts. She never stole people-food and instead preferred to hunt and gather outside. She always surprised us on hikes, as she would be just trotting along and then suddenly pounce into the tall grass like a cat, emerging with an unlucky field mouse. Once she even chased down and tackled a full-sized mule deer! Thankfully she didn't hurt it, or more likely get hurt herself, but she had remarkable drive, agility, and speed...just go ask the family of raccoons that tried to attack Bongo! Those eyes and those big "bat" ears were always tuned-in.

If dogs can have type-A personalities, Jane certainly had one. She reveled in challenging herself and would often choose the most difficult option just to prove she could do it. She could climb up and down ladders (head first!), and she'd scale large boulders rather than go around them. She got me into trouble with the Boulder Humane Society one day when she scaled a tree, jumped the backyard fence, and got nabbed by animal control.

Our move to Boulder also revealed that Jane was a water dog. I assumed my Golden, with his webbed-feet, would be the water dog in our family, but Jane proved me wrong. True to her personality, Jane wasn't interested in testing the water. Instead she would leap at least five feet horizontally from the shoreline into the water. Jane didn't fetch on land, but in the water she would swim as far and as fast as necessary to get a stick or ball. This unstoppable dog jumped off ledges and even dived, yes, dived, off diving boards.

Instinct and ability aside, what truly made Jane stand out was her love and loyalty. Shepherds are working dogs, and that term is not taken lightly. Jane's mission was to watch over her pack, and she accomplished that goal her whole life. Out of all the dogs who have been a part of my life since childhood, I have never had a dog who exhibited unconditional love like Jane. Even in her old age, keeping tabs on all of us and making sure we were okay was paramount.

You were probably wondering about all the teaspoons of peanut butter I mentioned earlier, and that's where this tale comes to a sad end. Years ago Jane was diagnosed with a disease called *degenerative myelopathy*, which over the course of her life would render her paralyzed. Controlling this disease required medication twice daily, so the peanut butter made it as pleasant as possible. After years of pain management, the disease finally caught up with Jane, and her quality of life really began to suffer. Before things became too troublesome for her, we made the difficult decision to let her go with the dignity she deserved.

Like Bongo before her, Jane led an incredibly happy and fulfilled life. She traveled all over Ireland and crisscrossed the United States at least six times. She hiked, skijored, and swam in pools, rivers, creeks, lakes, and oceans. She had her own condo in Winter Park (the glorified "dog house," as it was called), and just about every car we purchased was with her comfort in mind.

Who would have thought that the annoying dog on the street corner would turn out to be the most loyal, obedient, loving, protective companion imaginable? I'm so glad "that kind of dog" followed us home that day. Our lives would not have been so rich without her.

 *Bill Adkins*

Hamster Herding

Jetta was relinquished when her owner was surprised by the fact that German Shepherds get "large" (80 pounds). She came into rescue and was un-adopted twice, which led me to raise an eyebrow. Nevertheless, I inquired and was told she was returned because of her "antics."

Antics sounded manageable, so Jetta came to live with us. It turns out Jetta's antics are unique but completely tolerable. Some may even go so far as to call them cute. She loves going for walks around the neighborhood, and if she decides that

I am stopping too long to talk with neighbors, she takes the leash in her mouth to pull me along. She is particularly fond of plastic water bottles, but only if they have the tops screwed on. She carefully unscrews the top and then crunches the bottles—helpful for recycling! She also knows how to use her paw and snout to turn doorknobs and open doors. Once, when she was put in the bedroom while the pizza man delivered, she apparently tried to open the door but locked herself inside instead!

We call Jetta the "herdmaster" because she takes shepherding very seriously. One of her favorite "herdlings" was our hamster, Jessica, who escaped her cage on a regular basis. Jetta understood that nipping at a hamster's heels wasn't the proper herding technique, so instead, we would come home to find Jetta standing over Jessica after having licked her into a corner. Jessica was wet but unharmed. Jetta also tried herding one of my cats, who was terrified of her. It was classic miscommunication: the cat hid under the bed covers, meowed menacingly, and swatted at Jetta with her paw. Jetta was so thrilled the cat "liked" her so much that she promptly paid the cat even more attention.

Jetta's antics sometimes get her into trouble, and when she knows I am mad at her, she stays out in the backyard until my son comes home. Jetta doesn't spend much time in the yard anymore, though, because she hasn't done much to upset me since we adopted a second German Shepherd. We thought Jetta needed someone other than the cat to play with, so we brought Tillie home one day. The two of them got along great at their first meet-and-greet, and Tillie jumped in the car before we had even completed her adoption paperwork. The one *little* thing the rescue forgot to tell us was that Tillie had a bad case of diarrhea! She pooped three times in the back of our station wagon before we got halfway home. Jetta assessed the situation quickly and jumped in the front seat with us, making sure we knew she was not the offender. What a day!

Jetta and Tillie have been together for four years now. Jetta is well-behaved, and as strange as it may seem, every time there is a "dog offense," Tillie is the culprit. Or maybe Jetta has perfected her antics so much that she can just let Tillie execute them for her, leaving her without any blame...

 *Shirley Worthington*

Hurricane Heartbreak

Hurricane Katrina: Those two words still evoke sadness and disbelief in the American people. Animal lovers were further depressed at the overwhelming suffering endured by untold numbers of animals along the Gulf Coast. Even though I made two trips south to volunteer in the temporary shelters, my husband and I felt the need to do more; donations of money and time simply did not seem to be enough. Additionally, we were still suffering from the loss of one of our adopted German Shepherd Dogs who had recently died at the advanced age of fifteen. So I started looking on Petfinder.com to see if there was a German

Shepherd Dog who needed a post-Katrina home. Because our two surviving dogs were both old males, we were looking for a senior female.

I kept coming back to the North Louisiana German Shepherd Rescue website, which had an eight-year-old, female Katrina rescue named Prissy. However, she needed to be placed with her older male companion, Foto, and we did not feel another male would be a good addition to our family. Then one day I saw a notice that the old male had succumbed to the physical damage he had suffered in the long aftermath of the hurricane. Sad as it was, Foto's passing opened up the possibility for us to give Prissy a happy home.

Prissy had lived with three other German Shepherd Dog companions in New Orleans. When the levees broke, two of the dogs drowned, but Prissy and Foto were able to swim to a balcony. Nevertheless, this safety was an illusion. When the waters receded, the dogs became trapped on the balcony for almost three weeks before being rescued and reunited with their guardian. But their guardian no longer had a home and had no choice but to surrender the dogs to a rescue organization. I can only imagine how difficult that decision must have been, since she had already lost everything, but I am grateful she loved her dogs enough to put their needs first.

When I met Prissy I was impressed by her soft, almost ashy coloring and her prominent Roman nose, which was so similar to our dog who had recently died. Her ears were a surprise as the tips had been eaten away by flies, but this only added to her character. Prissy apparently liked what she saw, also, as she came directly to me and lay down for tummy rubs. She was obviously confused about loading into an unfamiliar car with a stranger and driving for several hours, but she took it all in stride—it was just one more upheaval in her life.

And so, Prissy joined our pack in Tennessee. The boys accepted her immediately, and she easily took to the slow pastoral life, navigating the dog door and exploring the woods. She protected her stuffed toys by burying them deep under bushes, with just the tip of an ear or a nose exposed so that she could pull them out when she wanted them. She snuggled with her new brothers and politely offered humans a paw in exchange for a pat. She had her issues, of course; she was afraid to go outside in the dark and barked frantically at storms with high winds. The thunder, which had worried almost every other German Shepherd Dog with whom we have ever lived, was not an issue for Prissy, but blowing rain and wind—that was another story. She even reacted so adversely to a TV documentary about Hurricane Katrina that I had to mute the sound when the hurricane winds were blowing. But these fears gradually abated, and Prissy began to look to her new brothers to determine what was really dangerous in her strange new world, such as dinner being late or a toy being lost.

Prissy came to us with very weak hips and muscle deterioration in her rear legs, still she tottered along with the other old dogs. She loved lying in the grass in the warm sun, occasionally giving the squirrels a warning bark about the danger awaiting them if they dared descend from the trees. She was a vibrant presence in our lives for just over a year, and then the spark began fading from all the old dogs. They passed on in rapid succession, finally leaving just Prissy. Only two weeks after the second dog's death, we awoke to find Prissy trying to crawl to the dog door, and even when we lifted her, she could not stand. It was time to say goodbye.

I still think about Prissy and the year we had together. Her presence was a gift for my husband, for our other dogs, and for me as she filled the space left vacant by our previous aristocratic female. I sometimes wonder if the loss of her two adopted brothers was more than she could bear after losing her initial family, her canine siblings, and her home. But, even if that is true, I know she was happy to be with us in her last year of life. She was safe and loved, and I am glad that she had a year of peace and sunshine. Although our time together was short, every minute was precious.

Though the urgency of Hurricane Katrina has passed, there are still many animals along the Gulf and all across the country who are in need of good homes.

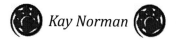 *Kay Norman*

Beating the Odds

S everal months ago a dirty guy reeking of alcohol dropped off his German Shepherd mix, Max, at the pound where I work as an animal control officer. Admitting he made Max live outside, he said he no longer wanted the dog because he kept getting hit by cars.

As soon as I laid eyes on Max, I was in love, and the more I found out about his situation, the angrier I became. There was obviously something wrong with Max's back end because his nails and the tips of his toes were worn off and gushing blood from being dragged during his 1½-mile walk to our facility. The guy went on and on about how his neighbors had to feed Max because he couldn't afford dog food while I tended to

Max's wounds, exhaustion, and thirst. I was shocked and saddened to find that Max had suffered for four years in the hands of this man. I tolerated his babbling for a few minutes until he raised his hand to Max, and Max cringed right to the floor. I was done, so I asked the guy for the $50.00 surrender fee to get him out of my office. He told me he would have to walk to the bank to get it and complained about the heat. Could he come back another day? *No!* I took his dog *and* his wallet and told him to take a hike. I wanted him to suffer, just as he had made Max suffer.

The guy did come back, paid the 50 bucks, and Max was officially free of him. Over the next several weeks, Max made himself at home in my air-conditioned office on a nice, soft, clean blanket atop his Kuranda bed. We gave him as much food and water as he wanted. Whenever I got up from my desk, poor Max got up to follow. It pained me to watch him walk.

I tried to get a rescue to take Max in, but everyone was either full or they wanted to know what was wrong with him. Finally, after almost losing hope, Barbara from Hot Water Rescue agreed to spring him and help me pay for his vet care while I rehabilitated him. After almost a month at the pound, Max was finally going to be a family dog. Our apartment is on my boyfriends' parents' 30-acre farm, and they are kind enough to let me bring home animals from time to time. It's a nice environment for Max, with other dogs, cats, ponies, donkeys, horses, chickens, pigs, etc. to keep him entertained.

It was also time to begin getting Max the vet care he desperately needed. Tests and x-rays confirmed that Max had perfect hips, which was the only good news. He also had heartworm and *Chronic Degenerative Radiculomyelopathy*

(CDRM—a progressive spinal cord disease). There is no cure for CDRM and no treatment. It just gets worse over time, eventually affecting Max's ability to walk. In a month or months (the vet couldn't tell), I would have to put Max down.

Or maybe I wouldn't...

Extensive online research revealed that many dogs with CDRM remain mobile by using a wheeled cart to support their back end. So after collecting donations to help with Max's vetting, I still had enough money left over to buy his dog cart. Poor Max was such a trooper while my boyfriend, Tim, and I sized it to fit and then strapped him in. At first Max didn't know what to do, but within minutes he had the hang of it and was off down the driveway. His first stop was to greet Tim's dad, and then he was off to say hello to our pony and donkey. Again on the move, he made another stop at the wood-splitting area to hang out with all the guys. Everyone was so happy to see him out exploring without dragging himself from spot to spot.

I can now take Max out for long walks, and he no longer has any pain. He simply rolls along in his cart with booties to protect his feet from sores. I actually have to put him on a leash because otherwise he'll take off down the ¼-mile dirt driveway to see whom he can greet first; he just loves everyone.

When I brought Max home, I wanted to show him what being loved, and cared for, was all about, even if our time together would be limited. Little did I know that Max would show me that even in the face of adversity, a little ingenuity can help one beat the odds, at least for a time.

 *Cari DeLorenzo*

Shepherd Shorts

Applause! Loud noises and unsettling events would set off Annie's sensitive colon like a latte machine. I usually managed to patch her up with doggie Kaopectate and Loperamide, but when I occasionally couldn't get to her in time, she fragrantly let her concerns be known on our white carpet. We always left Annie in the yard when unsupervised, until one day I got wrapped up in holiday preparations and jumped into the shower without thinking. The fact that Annie was still inside hit me with such horror that I ran out of the shower and through the house, putting her in the yard without even grabbing a towel. The dogs were fine. The house was fine. And so were my in-laws, who applauded (good thing Annie was out of earshot). They had apparently already arrived. –*Anonymous*

The Perfect Prewitt: When we first met Sweetie she was timid, but as soon as the kids jumped onto their battery-powered vehicles in the backyard, she went into herding mode! That day she did a great job of "keeping the kids out of harm's way," and ever since we adopted her she has been Lily's pillow, Mitch's soccer goalie, Mom's everyday companion while the kids are at school, and Dad's shadow. Sweetie is much more than a family *pet*…she is a family member. -*The Prewitt Family*

No Padlock Needed

oy, my days were numbered! My former owners had turned me over to animal control because....well, because. I had only lived outside and didn't meet many people, so I didn't know what to do when I found myself inside a small cage with all these people looking in at me. I decided it would be best to show them my tough side, so I growled and snarled a lot. The tough guy act worked, maybe a little too well, because before I knew it, there was a big padlock and a sign I couldn't read on my cage, and *nobody* was going near me.

That is, nobody except this one man who came and sat outside my cage and talked to me. I put on my best "back off!" display, but he didn't go away. Then one of the officer-ladies (who obviously believed me about how tough I am) hesitantly came and unlocked my cage. She told the man he was wasting his time; I was going to be put down that same day. He didn't seem to care, and I wondered, "Down where?"

The man came in and tried to put a rope around my neck. It seemed he wanted to take me out of the cage, so I figured I'd let him. Anything that wasn't the cage was fine with me! The two of us, along with another lady, went over to a small pen, where they let me sniff around and handed me treats. I didn't know what they were trying to pull, so I still acted all tough. Then I heard the man say, "We're taking him home," and I got really hopeful for the first time in days.

WOW! What a difference a day makes. Now I am the happiest dog on the block. I have this really super girl-dog to play with all day, I get to go in or out of the house whenever I want (I'm really interested in the "in" part), and I get to snuggle with my people on the couch. Plus, I get lots of treats, especially when I do something easy like sit or lie down (which I do anyway, silly people!).

My people keep bringing other dogs home and telling me to be sweet to them because they are "fosters." From what I've seen, "foster" means the other dogs go and I stay (woo-hoo!). I've gotta feel a little bad for the buggers, though; my people say they all go to good homes, but in my experience the best home is here! Could there really be someplace better? No matter. I've got my people, my buddies, and a home with no padlock required. If there's a heaven on earth, this is it!

 *Teddie, translated by Gale Hull*

Walks on Water

We were taking advantage of a warm Colorado January day, getting some fresh air and strolling at an outside mall, when there it was…a Lurcher. I grew up in England, where Lurchers are common, but this was only the second Lurcher I'd seen here in 30 years of living in America.

I had always wanted a Lurcher, which is typically a sight hound crossed with some type of herding dog. Often considered the gypsies' dog, "Lurcher" is derived from the Romany (gypsy) word *lur*, meaning *thief*, and *cur*, the English word for *bastard* or *mongrel*. "Lur cur," or Lurcher, thus means a stealing bastard, which is arguably appropriate as they were developed for poaching. They hunted deer, hare, and rabbit, and their bloodlines can go back many generations. Lurchers have great speed and endurance—think Road Runner meets Energizer Bunny—and are now used mainly for lure coursing, which is an event testing a dog's speed, endurance, agility, and hunting by sight ability.

This particular Lurcher was obviously a Greyhound/German Shepherd mix, given his color (brindle: black on tan) and build. At the mobile pet adoption trailer, he was introduced to us as "Tipsy." The name suited him well since he had lost the top half of his left ear and walked with the quasi-swagger of a barroom brawler (or a young dog who hasn't yet grown into his long legs).

I knew I had to have him, but at the time we were definitely NOT in the market for a third dog. We already had two rescue dogs—a magnificent, old, big, brindle (tan on black) mongrel called Rufus McGee, who was almost 14 ½, and a nine-year-old Border Collie/English Setter princess called Miss Chutney. A third large dog, young and full of energy, was more than we could handle. And even though a young playmate would have been good for Chutney, we worried about Rufus. While his spirit was still young, his body was slowing down, and one alpha dog was quite enough.

Rufus was the first dog my husband and I adopted together, so he held a special place in our hearts, and we were very respectful of his dignity. The bottom line is that even though I fell in love with Tipsy, we walked away....well, sort of. We actually went back to the mobile pet adoption unit to see about filling out paperwork, but the truck had packed up and gone back to the shelter.

Over a month passed, and as I talked to my stepmother in England about the rare Lurcher I couldn't quite forget, my eavesdropping husband checked the website and found "Tippy" was still up for adoption! (Apparently his name was actually "Tippy" due to the white tip on his tail. The name wasn't nearly as original as Tipsy, but I guess it was still fitting.)

We were horrified; we'd left Tippy to languish in the kennel for too long, so throwing all practicality to the wind, we pledged to go get him the next weekend. I vacillated between joy for Chutney and terror for Rufus and me. How was I going to manage their individual needs?

I checked the website many times each day to ensure Tippy was still posted, and then the day finally came. It was like Christmas; I woke before dawn and wanted to be at the shelter right then. As I lay there, his new name came to me in a flash—TWIGLET! "Twiglets" are my favorite savory English snack, and his brindle marking matched the snack exactly. Plus he was a Lurcher, an English dog.

When we arrived, Twiglet was nowhere to be found. As my heart sank, we were informed that he was quarantined with kennel cough. Lovely. We were also surprised to find that he hadn't been at the kennel for six weeks; he'd been adopted out...and returned! Gracious, what could he have done? Well, we later heard that he was not housetrained, sat on the furniture, and was destructive. I think he barked, too. Twiglet's saving grace was that he did not jump fences (a Lurcher skill).

Awful though he sounded, I knew it was not him. The people who'd adopted him had left him alone for 8-10 hours a day and not spent time training him. His behavior was on them. So I went on hoping we would sail through the interview, which we did. It seemed a bit strange that everyone was so enthusiastic and slightly surprised Twiglet was going to a home, and it wasn't until after we adopted him that I found out why.

During Twiglet's first trip to our vet, we found he has a liver condition. So I checked back in with the shelter and finally got the full story about Twiglet's life, which was not good. He was transferred in from another state and had been in and out of the shelter for most of his life, suffering from illness much of the time. We worked to get him healthy, but it was months before we got good liver tests back from the vet.

As predicted, Twiglet's bad behaviors were because of his previous owners, not because of the dog. We housetrained him in a weekend, and he learned everything as fast as we could teach him. While the first few weeks were not without drama (it was immediately apparent he had no boundaries, discipline, or manners), all Twiglet needed was consistency and kindness. If anyone had tried to train him in the past, it would have shown, but at least he was a quick learner.

Twiglet had obviously been punished when told to "come," as that was the hardest thing for him to learn. But it was all a matter of trust, which he'd learn from Chutney's example. Twiglet would come on his own accord, but not when asked. It took weeks before he really knew we would not harm him, and that time is now a distant memory. His heart is as big as a house, and he follows us everywhere all the time, seeking attention, sharing humorous antics, and fetching toys on command.

To our relief, Twiglet was great with Rufus. He was gentle, respectful, and playful, while letting Rufus be the dominant dog. They had six weeks together before Rufus was put down at home with us and the dogs by his side. Twiglet is devoted to Chutney, who taught him how to swim. It took four days as neither Greyhounds nor German Shepherds are known as water dogs, but Twiglet is now a fish, and they will swim together for hours.

Twiglet is a high-energy dog who needs a job, so we hike with him off leash 3-5 times a week. He is an AKC Canine Good Citizen, and he recently passed the training course to become a therapy dog through American Humane and the Delta Society's Pet Partners program. As with most Lurchers, Twiglet is incredibly devoted and affectionate. The Grayhound in him loves soft furniture, and the German Shepherd part gives him endurance and a smart mind. It is a most wonderful combination.

My husband and I are constantly amazed how this beautiful, loving creature was so maligned and endured such an awful life before he came to us. As his photo shows, he can walk on water and do no wrong.

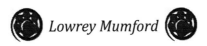 *Lowrey Mumford*

Giving It All to Chance

When we lost our beloved Brandy we desperately needed to hear the sound of four paws in our house once again, so we adopted Chance, and from the start our baby was off and running. After all, he was only *seven weeks old*! We attempted to confine him to the kitchen with a kiddie gate, but that didn't work. He climbed the gate and landed on the other side with a loud "kerplunk." (I swear he was giggling!) Another gate placed on top of the first one finally solved the problem.

To potty train Chance we put newspapers in front of the kitchen French doors, and he caught on right away. However, once the papers were soiled from end to end he would bark to let us know he needed clean papers. This usually occurred around 3am. Having Chance was like having a baby, and we each took turns getting up during the "wee" hours of the morning (pun intended). Oh my, the red and swollen eyes!

We planned on remodeling the kitchen later in the year, but when Chance got wind of the idea, he thought he would try to save us some money. He ripped up sections of the linoleum floor, bit off big chunks of the windowsill, and ate the cabinet corners. I told him the remodeling plan was down the road, but he continued trying to help—like the one Saturday he chewed a big chunk of the sheetrock out of the kitchen wall while we were still sleeping. Our clue to his early morning antics was the white chalk all over his face and mouth, making him look like a mad dog. The stern talking to we gave him didn't do much good; shortly thereafter he went right back to his remodeling. A TV tray in front of the hole finally ended Chance's mad dog exploits.

To say Chance was spoiled is an understatement. He was the only doggie in the neighborhood with his own kiddie pool, which he wouldn't get in! In fact, he would have preferred we return the thing to Wal-Mart, until one day his buddy, Jake, came over and hopped right in. Suddenly Chance wanted in, too, but it wasn't big enough for both of them! Jake told Chance, "I'm not moving, kid. You've got to wait your turn." But from that day forward, Chance thought that pool was the best thing ever.

Chance wasn't interested in lying on the floor. Any time we told him to "have a seat," he found a chair, sofa, or recliner. So instead of moving him off the furniture we got him his own La-Z-Boy. Actually he took my husband, Drew's, so we bought Drew a new one. I had my sofa, Chance had his recliner next to me, and Daddy Drew had his recliner on the other side of Chance's.

There was just one problem with the new seating arrangement: Now Drew didn't have a lamp. Since Chance had never requested a newspaper or other reading material, he didn't need a light, so it only made sense to rearrange the recliners. Well, when Chance came in and observed the new recliner placement, he didn't think much of it. He tried getting into Drew's recliner and was shooed away, so he went back to the bedroom to pout. Chance was so upset that he refused to return to the den until we had moved the recliners back.

After dinner Chance's favorite treat was "Frosty Paws" doggie ice cream cups, especially in the summer. He would sit in his bed, hold the cup between his front paws, close his eyes, and lick himself into oblivion. If a burglar had broken into the house during "Frosty Paws" time, Chance would have just told him to take what he wanted; life was too heavenly to care!

The amount we spoiled Chance was only matched by the amount of love he had to give. When Chance's grandmother (my mother) suffered a stroke, she came to live with us for the last nine months of her life. Her semi-catatonic condition was precarious, and Chance, her favorite, wanted her to come back so badly each time she was taken to the ER. The last time the ambulance returned her to our home, I let Chance see her after I got her settled in. I put down one bedrail, and he put both paws up on the side of the bed, stretched his neck, kissed her on each cheek, and then planted a big, sloppy kiss directly on her lips! He just wanted to let her know he was there and that he was going to make sure I took good care of her.

My baby, Chance, crossed over the Rainbow Bridge at the exact age of 13, but as you can tell, Chance was and is a very special part of my life. Singer Shania Twain said, "It's important to give it all you have while you have the *chance*." She may not have meant our Chance, but she nailed it—we gave him our all, and he gave it right back. He filled the void left by the death of my heart dog, Brandy, and always kept us on our toes.

 *Diane Ferguson*

Happy Jack

Talk about being left alone. Both of Jack's parents had passed away, his boy had gone to live with relatives, and his companion dog had been adopted out. Coastal White German Shepherd Rescue was having trouble finding a home for Jack since he was 11, mostly blind, and had hip dysplasia. Nevertheless, his ad caught my eye because it spoke of his undying spirit in the face of such adversity. I had recently lost my own 11-year-old White German Shepherd Dog to cancer and thought Jack would be the perfect fit in my home.

Right away Jack proved me right. Although blind and disabled, nothing seemed too daunting. Whether it be negotiating a strange house, walking through unfamiliar woods, putting up with an overly-enthusiastic 1½ year old German Shepherd constantly in his face, or serving as a pillow for my four-year-old daughter, Jack accepted everything with a big grin. He quickly assimilated into our household over the next few weeks, and my love and respect for him grew. Here was a dog who had been through so much (both physically and mentally), yet he was loving and affectionate, always laying his head against my chest for a hug. Jack was independent, too. When we got a big snowstorm he would routinely fall down in snow banks, but he didn't need help. He would just pick himself up and walk on, and through it all he had a smile on his face—my Happy Jack.

Jack's positive attitude was sorely tested when he bloated after just four months with us. Even as an old dog, Jack had such a love of life that when offered the choice of risky surgery or euthanasia by the emergency vet, I chose surgery. After three touch-and-go days, I brought him home. My husband felt I had gone too far in treating Jack since he was totally incapacitated, but within 48 hours my husband was eating his words! Jack was following me around the house, refusing help when he had to go out, and shortly thereafter, trotting around the yard, playing with our other dog, and even tolerating our new, four-month-old, White German Shepherd Dog puppy, who considered Jack his hero. Most importantly he had on his grin—my Happy Jack was back!

We had Jack for 15 months when his hip dysplasia got the best of him. His hind legs gave out, but he was still so happy and wanting so badly to be independent that I brought him to be fitted for a custom cart. He took to the demo right away, cruising around the parking lot with that old grin plastered on his face. It would take two weeks to have his cart built, and I couldn't wait to see him tooling around the yard in it, chasing the other dogs.

Sadly, Jack never got to use his cart. A week later I noticed his breathing becoming labored one night. I made him comfortable and lay down next to him, patting and reassuring him when he got scared. I must have dozed off for a few minutes when I felt a cold nose and gentle lick on my cheek. I thought it was my other dog, but when I rolled over, she wasn't there. I listened and all was quiet. I turned to look at Jack, and he was still. Jack had passed away.

I like to think it was his angel telling me goodbye with a gentle kiss. I know my Happy Jack is now running and playing and looking down on me from the Bridge with, of course, a big grin on his face.

 *Laurie Tylaska*

Dad's Midnite Beauty

Three female humans and a slew of animals always required Dad's attention. He met our tears over fallen sparrows, homeless dogs, and suffering goldfish with a resigned determination to make things right. His long shifts as a truck mechanic paid the vet bills, but it was Mom who always said yes. Whether it was, "Yes, we can keep the limping dog on the front steps," or, "Yes, we can bring the wheezing guinea pig to the vet," Mom was always more than willing to accommodate our pets' needs. Often it was Mom herself who had coaxed a fragile creature into a box, the car, or even the house. Dad was the one who got stuck hauling a shovel to the garden when tragedy stuck our little menagerie. As he oversaw a rodent funeral or witnessed a bird's final breaths, he was stoic and sensible.

That is, until Dad went to work one spring evening and caught a glimpse of the German Shepherd whom would one day be named Midnite, both for her jet black coat and because it was the shift he worked. The young stray ran with a pack in the rough neighborhood on the border of Brooklyn and Queens. Dad's company had a big lot in the run-down ghetto; the pack stumbled upon the respite it provided from aggressive gangs and relentless traffic, and the thin German Shepherd caught Dad's attention. She was only about a year and perhaps already pregnant, so while her companions journeyed on, she showed up again the next night. Dad threw her some scraps of his mid-shift meal, but the pup refused the food until he'd backed away. When she determined his distance was safe, her dainty face, its tan mask framed in thick onyx fur, dipped to devour the scraps.

This quickly became routine, and as summer wore on, trust between the expectant mom and my blue-collar dad grew like the dandelions that dotted a nearby vacant lot. She still shied away from physical contact, but eventually she ate from her favorite mechanic's hand. Progress was slow, but he was in no rush. When leftovers were determined insufficient and unwholesome, Dad bought a bag of dry dog food, which he stored in the trunk of his car.

Midnite soon gave birth, but only two of her pups survived. She nursed them in the lot that was now her home until they were eventually adopted by Dad's coworkers. The tiny furballs were secured in sedans bound for the suburban splendor that ensured fences to keep them safe, children to provide companionship, and even fireplaces to assuage the winter that posed a distant yet formidable threat.

When a rainy weather pattern hit New York, Dad let Midnite sleep in the cab of one of the broken trucks. After a few nights the supervisor complained and forbade him to allow the stray on company property. Dad denied his actions despite telltale black fur on the upholstered truck seat and continued to share meals with Midnite. My sister and I had grown used to his updates and often teased him, "Did you have another late-night rendezvous with your exotic beauty?"

A few times we asked why he didn't just bring her home, but she'd been deemed unadoptable. "One of the guys took her home, but she went nuts. She tore the blinds off the windows, ate through walls. She can't be domesticated."

We accepted that response until late in the autumn, when Dad was summoned to jury duty. He'd planned on leaving the food with a fellow mechanic who also had a soft spot for Midnite, but on Dad's last night of work before jury duty, the supervisor came down hard about the stray. When the boss threatened to contact animal control, Dad called home. He told Mom, "I know they'll put her down if they catch her. She'll act aggressively out of fear."

My sister and I hovered next to the phone as Mom simply said, "So bring her home." He reiterated his concerns, but Mom had an answer for everything. "So she'll live outside. You'll build a great doghouse, with heat and everything. Maybe she'll come around."

We jumped up and down excitedly, anticipating another family member. But Dad was quick to dampen the mood.

"You know, girls, she isn't like the other dogs. She's not going climb in your bed and wear cute bandannas. She may never even live in the house."

When morning finally arrived and Dad's car pulled into the driveway, we called our two rescued Lhasa Apsos into the yard, where everyone could meet in an open area. Midnite was very timid at first and stuck by Dad's side rather than explore her new surroundings. She shyly ducked her head when we petted her, but we caught a glimpse of intuitive eyes that held deep-rooted fear but also a glimmer of hope. It was obvious why Dad had worked so tirelessly to earn her trust; the dog was regal, even with her matted fur and bony midsection.

After a bath under the hose, she no longer smelled of diesel fuel, and she ventured inside the house a few hours later. When we finally stopped scrutinizing Midnite's every move, she climbed onto the sofa and fell fast asleep. My sister and I discovered her there, bony shoulders rising and falling in deep slumber, and called to Dad, "You have to come see the dog who may never live indoors."

Midnite's adjustment to domestic life was not always easy. For a while she had separation anxiety whenever Dad left. She shredded anything with his scent, especially slippers, and she often stared out the bay window with solemn eyes, awaiting his return. She took a long time to warm up to our extended family and even snapped at a few cousins. A rivalry grew between her and Shadow, our female Lhasa. After Midnite attacked Shadow and injured her severely, the two had to be separated whenever we left the house. Still, my parents didn't give up on the stray who had adopted Dad. To the four of us, she was a gentle companion yet fierce protector, and we respected that the issues she had were warranted.

As her tan muzzle became gray and her ribs no longer jutted out, we often teased Dad about his warnings. We'd cuddle up with the sixty-pound dog in a cute bandanna and remind one another, "This isn't like the other dogs, you know." For over ten years, Midnite knew neither fear nor hunger as she lived out her days on a sofa instead of asphalt. She passed away a long time ago after suffering from hip dysplasia. Though the steady parade of rescues has continued through my parents' house, Midnite is still the only pet Dad ever brought home, and none has claimed his heart like the regal German Shepherd who smelled of diesel fuel.

 *Michele Wallach*

It's All Johnny's

J ohnny came to us as my husband, Curtis', new K-9 partner. He was straight from Germany and obviously had never had any social interactions with other dogs. His life had consisted of training only.

My husband's instructions were that the job belongs to Johnny; the work truck belongs to Johnny; the salary is Johnny's. Johnny's job was much more important that Curtis'.

Border Patrol built a giant kennel in our backyard, which was meant to be Johnny's home. We were strictly advised that Johnny was government property and not to be treated as a pet: no walks, no car trips, nothing fun or doglike at all. Well, sometimes rules can be bent just a little, right?

Curtis' peers laugh at the fact that we have a collar and family ID tag on Johnny and actually let him live in the house. Over the years he has learned to tolerate, even like, our two rescued dogs and one cat. What's more, Johnny befriended a few of our countless fosters. Johnny is nine this year and showing his age. With a little arthritis settling in, we are counting on retirement for him soon. We can't wait until he is no longer "government property," and we can really show him how a dog's life as a family member is supposed to be!

 *Kendall Ganong*

Molly-B-Good

I always have to add a little something to a name, but my dog's name is Molly, and I have been her human for a year and a half (almost half her life). When we first met, we were both in need. I had just lost my three-year-old German Shepherd, Ashe, to kidney failure and couldn't stand going home to an empty house. Dinah (now Molly) had first been abandoned in the countryside and was then kept in a kennel for five or six months while waiting for somebody to love her.

Our first few weeks together were a challenge because Molly disliked other dogs, had little use for humans, dug at every chance, and spent endless hours chasing flies. As the days passed, I kept trying to figure out the puzzle that was Molly. She obeyed, knew all the basic commands, and wasn't possessive of her food. But when I looked at her, the eyes looking back were dull and lifeless. No spark, no communication. When I walked toward her she cowered all the way down to the floor. When I petted her she didn't respond, and she had no idea what a "treat" was.

The thought which kept running through my mind was, "Oh my, what have I done? This just isn't going to work." Yet I talked to Molly almost constantly. Every time I walked close to her, I reached out to touch her. When she cowered I stopped and petted her, trying to reassure her.

One day I came home and found she had attempted to dig to China, devastating my garden in the process. I turned around, got back into the car, and drove about while calming down and considering my options. I could tell the rescue group this just isn't working out and give her back to them. Or I could have a stronger, higher fence built around the garden. I opted for the fence.

A few more weeks passed, and then it happened. As Molly walked past me, I felt a cold, wet nose lightly brush against the back of my leg. It was the first time she had ever reached out to me. Learning to be "a dog" took more time, but today Molly's eyes sparkle with mischief. She greets me when I come home and dances me through the door, checking to make sure I haven't forgotten the way. She stops by the *special* cupboard door and waits patiently for her treat. When I am working at the computer, she slips her head under my arm and demands pets.

This Christmas a friend gave her a stuffed squeaky toy. She loved it, and whenever anybody came to the house, she ran to show them her toy. This is a huge improvement over the withdrawn dog who first entered my life. Molly doesn't chase flies much anymore, but she did just let a squirrel come into the backyard. What a difference from the summer day when she kept one treed for several hours.

Now when I look over at Molly snoozing on her bed, I think, "How could anybody not want her? She is such a puppy." Molly-B-Good? Sure she is. I wouldn't change her for the world.

 *Judy Broussard*

Shepherd Shorts

The Secret: Bill seemed like nothing more than a laid-back and loving German Shepherd, happy to have a new home. But our impression drastically changed the very next day when we received a call from our home security service alerting us that the door leading from the house to the garage had been opened. We immediately rushed home and opened the garage door to find no one else but our dog, Bill, wagging his tail in greeting. Incredibly Bill had somehow opened the locked, airline-approved crate we had placed him in fifteen minutes earlier, bending the metal frame and breaking the hard plastic...and then opened the door to the garage! That day we learned there was more to our pal Bill than met the eye. By night he was a family pet and by day a master of escape artistry! *-David Thompson*

Bad Cattitude: My foster dog, Jake, came to me with a bad catitude and chased my poor Pootie mercilessly! I tried to work with them, but since I am not a dog/cat psychologist, I ended up just keeping them separated. We all survived, and now Jake only has his own tail to chase in a new home where he no longer has a cattitude problem. *-Lisa Lombardo*

Buckin' Brujac

German Shepherds came into my life when I was in high school over 30 years ago. So when Chance died, it was only natural that I would seek out another German Shepherd. Our house was much too lonely without the sound of paws tapping across the floor.

I began my search online and discovered Alabama has its very own German Shepherd rescue located only about 15 miles from where I grew up in Wetumpka! Well, I started scrolling down the page ever so slowly, and at the bottom I found a picture of a baby German Shepherd. He appeared to have big ears and big feet, just like my Chance, and to my surprise, his name was Bru! I laughed and laughed because my husband's name is Drew, and my father used to call him "Bru" as a joke. Was that a sign or what?

I had to explore this further. After several phone calls, completion of the adoption form, a home visit, and a consultation, Mr. Bru was approved for our home. Adopting Bru was a process, and I remarked to my husband that it was probably easier to adopt a child than a dog.

The day of adoption finally came, and I must say, our first impression of Bru was a bit of a shock—he was so scrawny! I realize he was only six months old, but his picture made him look to be much larger. Bru's feet were so small in comparison to Chance's, whose were as big as baseballs. But Bru's ears were indeed big, reminding me of a jackrabbit.

Our new life together was an adjustment for everyone. We had forgotten what it was like to have a six-month-old puppy, as it had been 12½ years since Chance was a pup. It didn't take long for me to realize that I had to change Bru's name. It was too close to my husband's and he couldn't tell if I was calling him or the dog. Brutus or Bruno just didn't suit him, and I felt at a loss until one morning, as I was walking him, it came to me: Telly Savalas...starring as an incorruptible officer in the 1970's television drama *Kojak*... Jackrabbits... Brujac!

"Brujac" fit our new dog perfectly—a unique name for a dog who is truly an individual. For example, Brujac likes to go in reverse. He also does a bucking bronco impersonation after pottying. It's so entertaining that Drew has remarked we're only a saddle and monkey short of a rodeo act.

Though my other German Shepherds promptly chased cats out of the yard, one of Brujac's best friends is Tiger, the next door neighbor's cat. Every morning they greet each other with a kiss, and Tiger rolls over on his back for Brujac to do as he pleases. Brujac paws Tiger. Tiger paws Brujac. Tiger walks in and out of Brujac's legs.

Brujac's other best friend is Maggie, a Lab/Golden mix. Maggie is an "older woman" (three going on thirty), and when we go on our morning walks, Maggie is waiting for us at the end of her driveway. They have to play their staring game first, and then they're off with body slams and back rolls as they race around the yard. It's all fun and games until I have to call it off—after all, we do have a walk to complete. As Miss Scarlet O'Hara would say, "Tomorrow is another day."

Brujac likes to sleep on his back with all four legs stretched out stiff. His eyes are closed and his mouth is slightly open, showing off a grin that is similar to that of a possum.

Well, I need to close this dog and monkey show. As you can tell, I could go on and on about my Brujac; there's just so much to say. Our multi-faceted dog may be a master of impersonation, but we're not fooled. At the end of the day, he's always our Brujac, a beloved family pet.

 *Diane Ferguson*

You Have Chosen...Wisely!

As an animal control officer, one of my jobs is to check out kennels after the weekend and see what was brought in. On this particular day, I was sorry to see a tan male German Shepherd/Chow mix sitting there with a large gash on his front leg. He had been picked up as a stray by the police department and brought to the kennels to await his fate. No one reclaimed him as I worked through the day. That was not a good sign.

At the end of the day, I dutifully loaded him up in my truck to transport him to the shelter for medical attention and whatever fate awaited him. He had a big smile and a wagging tail. I hated that as I unloaded him and helped to process him. I named him Nick and put him in the run where he would wait for a vet visit at some point. He looked at me like, "Where are you going, old friend?"

Well, I kinda forgot about old Nick until I was walking past the kennels while putting a dog in another run. He was healed up and looked at me like I had not been gone five minutes, let alone a month! I walked up to Adoptions and asked what was going on with him. I was still kinda new, so maybe it was a ploy, but the adoptions person said normally they do not hold dogs this long, and he'd have to check and let me know.

I left that day feeling kinda bad, like I'd drawn the wrong kind of attention to Nick, so I promptly found an excuse to go back the next day. Nick was still sitting there. I asked him if he wanted to come home with me, and he perked them ears up with a big grin, like, "Oh yes!" I quickly filled out an adoption form, paid his bail, and got him neutered and updated on his shots.

The next day I walked into the shelter and told them to get me my dog! They thought I was crazy and told me to get him myself (which I promptly did) because they did not seem to believe I had adopted Nick. We had a great ride home, with him looking at everything (especially on my side of the truck). He met my two other dogs and everyone got along fine.

Nick has been a great dog ever since. He was one or two years old back then and is about seven now. We have had our moments, but who doesn't? We have also had many adventures! It's always fun when Nick lets me "abuse" him by dressing him up. Memorable costumes include "Nick the Gladiator" and "Indiana Nick," the latter of which earned him first prize at a Halloween rescue event. I am still happy to see them big ears perk up at mealtime as he waits to eat. He has me trained well—I say that magic word, "Eat," and Nick gets to enjoy. I often wonder why anyone would let him go.

 *Michael Antol*

Even I Can Change the World (for Someone)

I changed the world for Jones. When I met him at the shelter his name was "Stray," he was around 10 years old, and he was about to be euthanized. After he passed the Garden State German Shepherd Rescue (GSGSR) temperament evaluation (which consists of a variety of tests including staring, massaging, gentle tail pulling, putting a fake hand in a food bowl, taking away treats, introducing to cats/dogs, etc.), we knew we had to get him out of there quickly. So sad, old, dirty Jones became my first foster dog.

After two good scrubs in my driveway with a hose (he smelled *so* bad!) and a few days of quarantine in my basement for a terrible eye infection, Jones easily assimilated himself into our lives. This gentle, friendly, trained dog liked going for walks, but he was a little lame and struggled to get around the block. I discussed this with another GSGSR member, and she said to keep walking him. Since he was old, probably arthritic, and had been sleeping on a concrete floor for two weeks (and who knows what before that), the best things we could give him were good food, love, and some exercise.

When the time came for Jones to meet Roxy (my "forever" dog) and the cats face to face, they were already acquainted through the basement door. The transition was smooth, and Jones fit right in. He just walked around slowly, sniffed the cat, sniffed Roxy, and then parked himself in his bed, grateful for a comfy spot to rest his weary body.

After a trip to the vet for pain medicine and some joint supplements, Jones perked up a bit. He started to come out of his shell, playing with Roxy and slowly following Pootie (the cat) around. He was *so* interested in Pootie, but he was smart and knew to take it slow. His patience paid off and Pootie became his buddy.

It's hard to believe our perfect gentleman was abandoned. Jones was so gentle that I knew I could trust him with my pets and never felt the need to crate him. I like to think he had a happy home, maybe living with an elderly person who passed away or had to move in to assisted living. A dog as well-mannered as Jones doesn't just show up on earth at his age without having been loved and trained, so I'm sorry for somebody's loss.

After living with me for almost two months, Jones was adopted, but his rescue story didn't quite end there. The grandfather in his new family fell ill, and Jones became neglected. The situation got messy, but we miraculously found him the perfect home on the same day we brought him back into rescue, with a wonderful woman living near the Jersey shore. Now Jones spends his days walking on the beach and receiving endless attention and affection from his new mom and neighborhood kids.

Jones' "mom" has since become a new grandmother, and Jones is in charge of alerting people when he hears the baby cry. He is a good "nanny," and I can honestly say Jones is the best dog I've ever met. I miss him to this day.

 *Lisa Lombardo*

Bravery Barks

I was at work when I opened an email from a friend about a German Shepherd desperately needing help. The skinny dog named Haunna looked defeated—it was truly the worst case of sadness I had ever seen. Her face showed no hope, and her sadness touched me in a way that nothing ever had before.

The email stated Haunna had been the personal dog of a K-9 handler (law enforcement officer whose partner is a canine) in a very rural area of Southern Georgia. He had taken her to the local animal shelter requesting they euthanize her, but thank goodness the shelter staff did not. Instead they realized she was pregnant and gave her a little time to find help. The starved, sick girl gave birth to three stillborn pups while at the shelter. The email implored people to write letters asking for justice for Hannah. Her owner needed to be taken to task for his cruelty.

I could not get Haunna's face out of my mind, so I did more research. It turned out Haunna was also posted on the Germanshepherd.com urgent board, and there were many people trying to help her. Southern Cross German Shepherd Rescue needed assistance transporting her into their care in Clarkesville, GA, and a kind-hearted volunteer stepped up. Haunna, renamed Hannah, was finally free but in very bad shape, and the transport volunteer actually had to stop at a vet on the way to Clarkesville to control some terrible bleeding.

Once in Clarkesville, her skin infections were treated and her infected uterus and ovaries removed. Hannah also had two mammary nodules removed, which were regrettably never sent in for testing. Though the handler denied it, Hannah had obviously been used as a breeding machine and had suffered terribly. She was emaciated and had chipped teeth, which was likely from eating rocks or chewing on a wire cage.

The rescue paid for Hannah's treatment, and my partner and I supported them by bringing items Hannah needed. When I finally had the privilege of meeting Hannah in person, just seeing her take a chew bone made me cry. A piece of my heart stayed with Hannah when I left, and it wasn't more than a month before I was approved to adopt her.

In loving arms things were looking up, but the bad news seemed to keep rolling in. Hannah tested positive for heartworm and still needed treatment after I had adopted her. I had to raise $750 to help her, which was largely done with the help of wonderful friends, most of whom I've never met face to face in the Dogster.com community.

Finally Hannah was feeling great, and keeping her calm became the new challenge. It was months before she barked, which was the most wonderful sound I had ever heard. She didn't know how to play and had most likely never seen a toy, but she warmed up to a Nylabone Frisbee. When we threw her a big party to celebrate her health, you can bet that the toy she selected from the pet store was one of her favorite Frisbees.

Hannah still deserved justice, and I tried everything I could to make that canine handler take responsibility for his neglect. I repeatedly called the district attorney in his area (which was four hours away from me). The Georgia Bureau of Investigation took up the case, but that really only meant a dead end. I wrote letters, organized petitions, went to the media, and solicited our governor, who turned Hannah's case over to our Department of Agriculture (another dead end). Ultimately all charges were dropped.

Of course, I'm heartbroken that we cannot hold the handler accountable, but at least I can give Hannah a good life. She is still unsure of people, even friends, and baseball caps and clicking noises apparently bring back bad memories. Regardless, Hannah still continues to grow, and we see incremental progress all the time.

Some call her "Hannah the Brave," and that bravery has recently been tested again. It started as a black spot inside of her ear, which the University of Georgia College of Veterinary Medicine identified as melanoma. We also found two more mammary nodules; one turned out to be buckshot pellet and the other, cancer.

Even though our trips to the University have become frequent and costly, I cannot put a price tag on the joy I get from watching Hannah learn and grow. Despite all she has been through, she still has so much love to give. She's an impeccably-behaved companion, and her eyes just melt my heart. She's opened my closed eyes to the world of animal abuse and neglect and reminded me how many lose their lives each and every day for no good reason.

Because of Hannah, I have been a rescue volunteer for about a year and a half now. I do transport, email and post about animals in need, and participate in whatever other ways I can to help. In rescuing Hannah, Southern Cross German Shepherd Rescue saved her life *and* empowered me to help save many more.

 *Wanda Stover*

Play Boy

My husband was the first to have the idea to add a German Shepherd to our home. His grandmother had inherited one, and he loved its regal, calm nature. He thought the German Shepherd breed would be the perfect complement to our goofy, mixed-breed girl, Astor, so I immediately began searching the internet for a German Shepherd in need of a good home. What I found, unfortunately, was that the number of German Shepherds needing rescue was countless! It seems many people are attracted to this wonderful breed but not quite ready for the responsibility of such a keenly intelligent dog.

As I searched through one dog after another, one picture in particular caught my eye. Whether it was the goofy grin or the crooked ears I don't know, but I knew instantly that we'd found our German Shepherd! We contacted the rescue group, who said they'd saved Murphy from "death row" after he was found wandering the interstate with a rope around his neck. He was so malnourished and feeble he couldn't even climb our stairs for the first few weeks, not to mention he'd also contracted a pretty bad cold in the pound. Because of all his woes, Murphy was pretty lethargic for a one-year-old dog.

"Happily ever after" does exist, though. Over time Murphy gained strength and muscle mass. He now doesn't only run up and down the stairs, he flies, and he loves playing ball in the park. He's very intelligent, just as one would expect from a German Shepherd, and we can always dazzle the neighborhood kids with his tricks. Most importantly, he's a friendly, playful companion for Astor and a loving pet for us. He's not the stoic, noble dog we were first searching for— with his crooked ears and puppy energy—but we wouldn't have it any other way.

 *Rebecca & Alan Carroll*

Shepherd Shorts

A Difficult Road Is Easier When Traveled with Companions: I underwent gastric bypass surgery, conquered the 100-pound weight loss mark, and knew I needed a companion to walk by my side as I made my journey toward better health. A German Shepherd puppy on a shelter website stole my heart, and since his real life persona was as wonderful as his picture, I adopted him and named him Lucas. Lucas was then trained by a close friend who specializes in training military German Shepherds, and he's well on his way to becoming a strong, graceful dog. Becoming healthy has been a difficult road for me, but Lucas and my recently adopted, six-year-old Doberman/Lab mix fill me with the optimism I need to keep walking. -*Nicolie Lyles*

Bumbling Baron: His name is "Baron," but it just doesn't fit. This HUGE, one-year-old (or so), mostly German Shepherd Dog is the embodiment of goofiness. Watching him run is like seeing 85 pounds of confusion. He's a vertical miracle. He's got a tall, skinny body but a face only a mother could love: gummy eyes, one floppy ear, a big bucket head, and scars everywhere. He is just more of a "Gomer" or a "Goober" than a "Baron." Nothing but a big insecure puppy, he's unruly *and* as sweet as they come. -*Debbie Tomblin*

Mercy Me!

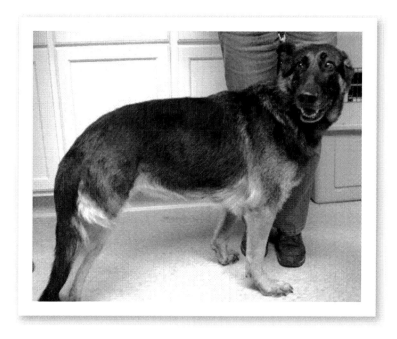

They say a picture is worth a thousand words, so picture a raw chicken leg that's been boiled to the point when the meat starts to pull away from the bone. That's what Mercy's right rear leg looked like from the ankle up. Oh, and don't forget to consider the smell. Yuck!

Mercy, this strong-willed, sweet, beautiful German Shepherd, was found alone and emaciated, wandering in the woods. Apparently her leg had been caught in a trap, and to avoid starvation, she it chewed off to free herself. Her horrible ordeal flashes a picture in my mind: the opening scene of the horror movie *Saw*, where one character is ankle-cuffed and forced to cut off his own foot to save his life. I don't know if this is something I could do, but in the face of death, God only knows. Mercy did what she had to.

This girl really needed our help, and we knew exactly what to do. We raised enough money in a week to properly amputate the remaining stump of a leg and pay for her post-surgical care. Anemic, starving, and fighting infection, we weren't sure if Mercy would even make it through surgery, but we knew we had to give her the chance to try. With a crew standing by to transfuse blood and administer subcutaneous fluids and pain meds, Mercy was sedated and surgery began. Dr. V, with Paradox Spay/Neuter, Inc., under advisement from Dr. Elizabeth Perry, began the arduous task of removing the hideous, gnawed, gnarly stump at the hip. Nearly three hours later, the surgery was complete with no transfusion needed.

It was evident that Mercy felt somewhat better immediately following surgery, and within an hour of waking up, she was already pottying outside. She spent the night in the hospital and was immediately put into foster care the next day. Due to Mercy's severe anemia, we fed her an extremely high protein diet consisting of steaks, eggs, peanut butter, and many other human-grade, protein-rich foods. She additionally went through several rounds of antibiotics to stave off infection.

Four months later, Mercy is doing well: running, playing, and still eating three high protein meals a day. She seems to be a happy girl, and now instead of horror movies, I'm just picturing the perfect forever home for her.

 *Melissa Christopher*

Dear Diary

S mall, smart, and sweet...that's me! Hi, I'm Hannah, and my foster mom says I'm as cute as they come. I have two switches: On and Off. When I'm "On," I'm very busy. Not in a bad way; I'm just a curious girl, sticking my nose everywhere and checking up on everybody and everything, just like a good German Shepherd should. But even though I'm "puppyish," I don't chew up stuff or ruin things—I just like to collect them. Lately I've been collecting my experiences in a doggie diary. Want to see?

November 5th

Everyone at my foster home likes me, even the old grouchy alpha dog, Sampson. He lets me lick his face and pounce on him. I love him and the kitty in my house, too. Sometimes we just lay there and look into each other's eyes. It's a good break from the chasing and running and tumbling. It doesn't matter that they are older and bigger because I'm tougher and faster. Can't catch me!

I still don't know about this "ball" thing the other dogs chase. It doesn't appear to be food, so why are they chasing it? Maybe I'll give it a try sometime soon, but it seems kind of silly.

These people are so easy here at my foster home. I've convinced them that I must sleep in the house instead of a crate or kennel, and my "sad puppy" face works wonders when I want a treat or chicken broth on my kibble. Suckers!

But even with the puppy face, they make me "sit" before getting a treat. What's up with that? I'm still fighting them on it, but if all I've got to do for a treat is put my bottom on the floor, I'll take it.

I've been growling at people I don't know because I'm not really sure what they're up to. My foster family keeps telling me to stop, but I'm only trying to protect myself. I guess I'll try and be a little more welcoming, but I'm still not sure if I'm taking their advice on this one.

I definitely can't complain in this home, but from what they tell me, having my own person or family would be great!

November 12th

Each morning I must check that all the trees in the yard are where I left them the night before and that the fence perimeter is in place. Then I check it all again—wouldn't want any trees getting away. Better check the other dogs, too. I wonder if they have any new "news" for me to read? Sniff sniff...

What a busy day! I get it now, that ball thing really *is* fun! It's still not food, but it's fun to chase the ball and compete with the other dogs for it. Did you know that some balls squeak? They're great!

November 18th

I'm tired because my roommate kept me up all night. I don't get it; we finally made it into the house to sleep (no more kennel), and he whined and paced for hours. There were lots of loud, scary noises, but get over it! We're *in* the house and they were *outside*, dummy. In here it's just cozy, spacious, and warm.

Yesterday my folks took me out for a drive. The car is so exciting because there is so much to look at and sniff when the window is down! We went to the store where my food lives, and it smelled so good. The only thing was that all these strange people insisted on talking baby-talk to me and petting me. Totally creepy...but I didn't growl. I think they all meant well.

Things were going along swimmingly until the super great car ride ended at that place where they poke you. First they got all in my ears, and now that we're home, my family is doing the same. Owww! They're sore enough already, so could you please stop sticking stuff in them? That stuff is *gooey*. People are so annoying.

Today's schedule: follow people around, look out of all the windows, check on the three other dogs, eye that cat, surf the countertops in the kitchen, nap, repeat.

November 22nd

Hey, you know how sometimes you walk past a window, and you see something you think is another dog, and so you have to bark at him, and then you figure out that you're just barking at yourself? Yeah, that happens to me sometimes, too. It happened today, and after realizing I was only looking at myself, I couldn't help but remark, "Wow, what an adorable dog. I'm even *cuter* than I thought!"

December 1st

Last night was the first night I got to sleep in the bedroom with the people and the two old dogs! (Sorry you're still in the mudroom, roomie, but that's what happens when you keep me up all night.) The cat got to sleep in bed with the people so I gave it a try, too. Unfortunately that was short-lived, and it was back down on the floor with the old dogs for me. Oh well, it was still warmer in there than outside.

Every day I exercise these old dogs, but the really old, fluffy one with the mask just didn't want to get with the program today. I offered my herding assistance by running around and nipping at his heels. *Note to self: Don't herd a Malamute.*

December 7th

It was big truck dumping gravel day at our house, and I wasn't having it. The old dogs didn't care much, but I told the truck to go away again and again. At least I'm a good guard dog! My warnings finally worked, and the truck left and never came back. But now there are lots of rocks and gravel here. What am I supposed to do with all of that? I hope the trees don't try to leave because it will probably take me a while to round them up. I'll check in on them tomorrow morning.

December 11th

What is going on here? The people let the cat on the chairs and sofa and even in bed. What about Hannah? Huh? I'm the one keeping track of your yard for you! Not fair.

December 17th

Last night when I was asleep *beside* the sofa (ehm...), a plastic rectangular thingy with soft rubber buttons fell on me. It said, "Chew me," but just as I started to take a satisfying crunch, someone reached down and grabbed it. Apparently it has something to do with that noisy TV. Humph.

December 23rd

I love Turke. That handsome guy is my favorite playmate although he gets noisy sometimes. I like to chase him, and then we roll on the floor and chew on each other... And everything is *just fine* until somebody gets a fang in the eye and starts yelping. Big baby.

January 4th

Last night the new dog here was causing a fuss. He was being rambunctious and trying to eat the cat. What a jerk! Our person finally held him by the collar and said, "Why can't you be as good as Hannah? See how calm and well-mannered she is?" Well, I don't think I've *ever* heard anyone say that before, and it just brought tears to my big, beautiful eyes. Not only am I gorgeous, I'm well-mannered, too!

I was so happy I decided to go tell the neighbors about it, so I walked right out the front door. I hadn't been out there without a leash before, and I guess I got a little too excited. My people called for me, but I couldn't hear them because I was too busy enjoying the scent of freedom. It wasn't until I ran across the street that I realized I was out and about *on my own*. Uh-oh. I started to panic, but I've got to hand it to those humans, they knew just what to do. They followed me in their car, and, when I saw them, I hopped right in. I think they were very upset, but I got a treat anyway.

January 9th

Today I got to go for a car ride again. Yeah! After driving for a while, we met someone who hugged on me and walked me and talked to me. She asked me if I would like to go home with her and be her best friend for the rest of my life. My decision was made the second she mentioned that I would be sleeping *in* her bed if I wanted! She also said something about playing on a beach, and it sounded so good that I kissed her right on her face. I think I was just adopted and am spending the rest of my life in Florida. I'll miss my temporary family—that big, furry guy, my other friends, and the nice people—but I'm diggin' this new adventure.

Hannah, translated by foster mom,

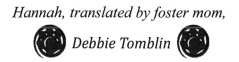 *Debbie Tomblin*

Paid in Full

Some idiot discarded Denny and left him for dead in one of the worst shelters in Texas. Apparently Denny kept chewing his way out of the yard, and his owner had finally refused to pay the escalating fines. When I saw Denny's pictures and story in a rescue email, I knew I had to save him. He was about to be euthanized, so I asked a friend to pull Denny from the shelter and take him to a vet (thanks Debra) while I sped across Texas to get him.

The first time Denny saw me he walked right up and carefully assessed me with his big, dark eyes. He then barked, as if to say, "What the heck took you so long?" He knew I was there for him, and he was so sweet. I was glad I had made the 13-hour round-trip drive to rescue him, even though the car ride home turned out to be only the beginning of Denny's long journey.

Denny tested positive for heartworm and had lost most of his hair from a bad flea infestation and allergies. He smelled *so* foul, even after a flea dip. He was full of intestinal worms and ear infections and his teeth were broken from chewing his way out of wherever he had lived. His vet bills were adding up, and the rescue couldn't afford them, so I decided to adopt Denny as my own.

Regardless of the costs of saving Denny, he paid in full with appreciation and love. He was one of the best dogs I'd ever had, and he never even thought of escaping *my* yard. He was a momma's boy for me and a buddy for Stella and Suzy (my two White German Shepherds), who loved him right back like he had been with us forever. It was truly meant to be.

Denny eventually died from anal sac cancer, but I feel good that I gave him what was probably the best five or six years of his life. By then Stella had passed, I had adopted another White German Shepherd named Chloe, and I was fostering a small, mixed-breed dog named Hermione (whom I ended up adopting). The "kids" and I had a little service for Denny, at which his pal Suzy sat with his body in the back of my van while I dug a hole. They all watched as I pulled his limp body from the van to the grave and covered him up. The whole thing was very sad, but we were all mourning and needed closure.

I will always miss you, my "Biggie Boy," but I'll see you at Rainbow Bridge, where I know you and my other fur kids who have gone before you await me. Thanks for sending me two more beautiful angels, Nicky and Nigel, to watch over me in the meantime.

 *Annmarie Mikelski*

A Perfect 10!

Dagwood is a "special needs" rescue, and he takes the "special" part to heart. He was bred for sale, but as he was the runt of a litter of 10, no one wanted him. It soon became clear to the breeder that Dagwood and some of his other siblings wouldn't be sold fast enough, so he dropped the remaining pups off at the animal shelter. German Shepherd Rescue of Central Alabama (GRSCA) took all of them, and a foster mother stepped in to provide the care they needed.

While the other pups grew normally, Dagwood didn't, and a veterinary specialist identified that Dagwood couldn't digest food properly. His prescription was simply an enzyme with every meal, which was something I could definitely handle. So when I saw him at one of the GSRCA fundraisers, I took him home to become the third in our pack.

Dagwood was almost a year old when I got him, and he weighed less than 35 pounds. He's now twice as old and weighs almost twice as much! He is a talker and makes a whistling sound when he is trying to communicate. A Dagwood yawn is like Southern speech—there are lots of syllables. He loves his two older, German Shepherd sisters, and for the first time enjoys being part of the pack instead of the outcast. That, to him, is special, and to us makes him a perfect "10!"

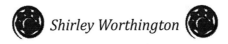 *Shirley Worthington*

Too Obvious to See

When I first met Shadow, I was with my foster dog, Ginger, at a Greater California German Shepherd Rescue (GCGSR) Adoption Day event. I had been attending these functions with Ginger for weeks with nary a "bite" of interest from a human in all that time. I didn't want to commit to adopting her myself, having too recently lost my Katy dog. I thought I'd just have Ginger as my foster dog forever, but then, out of nowhere, the perfect family walked up to the group of dogs and settled on mine. Before I knew it, we had completed the home inspection and signed the adoption agreement. *My* Ginger was gone.

This wasn't the first time I had felt like this about a foster dog. German Shepherds are such an amazing breed that it's easy to immediately fall in love with each one. Saying goodbye was just too difficult each time, so I made the decision then and there that my fostering days were over, or so I thought.

That same day Ginger was adopted, I had my first encounter with Shadow. She was an eight-year-old, skinny, bi-color German Shepherd Dog with glazed-over eyes that darted around and focused on nothing. I was told this homely dog needed to be walked, so as an act of mercy, I volunteered. I opened her kennel and out she bolted, dragging me behind her on a three-mile run. When we finally made it back, I happily returned her to her overworked foster mother, packed up my belongings, and went home—alone.

A week or so later I learned Shadow had attacked the family dog in her foster home, so my friend (and fellow foster mom), Mary, was asked to take her instead. But that didn't last long, either, because Shadow did not fit in with Mary's cats. Since I had no other animals in my home, Mary asked if I could take her "for just a little while," until they could find someone else to foster her. I reluctantly agreed, and she was delivered that afternoon. With all my previous foster dogs it was love at first sight, but this was not the case with Shadow, so I really didn't think much of it.

Shadow had no interest in developing any sort of relationship with me, and the feeling was mutual. You already know why I wasn't a huge fan of hers, and when I later learned of her history, her attitude toward me made complete sense, too. By the time Shadow had come to be with me, she had lost so much, so many times, that she had given up on her bid for a forever family.

Shadow walked through the front door that first day with the same glazed look, head down, scrawny, and totally aloof—unattached and unattachable. I had absolutely no interest in this unattractive mess of an unruly dog. I showed her how to use the dog door, where the water was, and where she could sleep; we then both went about our business.

Mary checked in on Shadow the next day while I was at work to be sure Shadow hadn't eaten my house. When she left, Shadow dug under the fence and was found by my neighbors, who secured her in their yard until Mary could pick her up. It would be a long time before Shadow and I warmed up to each other, but I was momentarily elated when I walked into Mary's house, and Shadow came running around the corner to greet me when I called her name. Perhaps she thought she had again been abandoned as she was obviously relieved to see me. It's hard to say what makes the connection between a human and a canine, but this event was the start.

Life went on the same for another few months. We'd wake up early, go for our run, I'd feed her, and then I'd leave for work. In the evening I'd return, walk and feed her, and then we would again go about our evening business separately. She'd accompany me on hikes and various trips each weekend, and we'd go to adoption events on Sundays. Each week we would watch all the puppies and young, lovely dogs get adopted, and then, of course, seemingly unadoptable Shadow would go home in the evening with me.

As the days, weeks, then months passed, our connection grew through just the familiarity of each other. Shadow was anticipating being moved to another foster home, and I was just waiting to find the perfect companion. Our bond grew so slowly that neither of us was able to recognize it, until one night, on my drive home, my mind went to Shadow, and I had a feeling of happiness; I found myself looking forward to seeing her. When I arrived at the back door she was, for the first time, there to greet me with a wagging tail. Our eyes locked and big grins spread across both of our faces. We had finally found each other.

Good things come in surprising packages, and, although my time with Shadow is more limited than it would have been had I fallen in love with a puppy, we'll be happily together until the end. I owe some, "You were right's," to the people who tried to point out that Shadow was already my dog, as I brought her week after week to Adoption Days, and I'm grateful to the families throughout her life who gave her up, time after time, because their loss was my gain. It took a while, but now we both know the companionship we were hoping for was right in front of us the whole time.

 *Terry Menshek*

No Trouble at All

Trouble was my first rescue dog, whom we adopted from Action For Animals. His litter of German Shepherd-mix puppies was saved by a cop who caught some jerk trying to dump them from his car into the woods. The man was arrested and the five-week-old puppies, still nursing from their mother, were taken into rescue.

Trouble weighed a whopping five pounds when we adopted him, but love and food nourished him into a 100-pound dog. He quickly earned his name at the shelter because even though he was tiny, he would jump over his littermates and escape from his pen. We kept this name even though Trouble was really no trouble at all.

This German Shepherd/Husky mix was a gorgeous boy with one blue eye and one brown eye. He was very smart and affectionate, and when he spoke I swear he was saying "I Wuv Woo." When Trouble joined our family he became the youngest of three, but then Sheba died from degenerative myelopathy. Trouble and I were both grief-stricken and mourning, and he did his best to comfort me.

Being a playful boy, I was surprised one day to see him favoring his left hind leg. His vet diagnosed it as a torn cruciate ligament, and the specialist convinced us that the TPLO (tibial plateau leveling osteotomy) procedure was best. Then just a few short months later, Trouble began favoring his other hind leg, so we again went to the specialist, who again performed a TPLO surgery.

I was very concerned because I had read that the TPLO can be associated with *osteosarcoma*, bone cancer. Though the specialist assured me that the odds of a dog developing osteosarcoma from this procedure were slim and that we'd know it was coming because a treatable bone infection would precede it, I couldn't shake my wariness.

Well, first Trouble's second surgery became infected. When antibiotics did not clear it up, he needed another surgery to remove the metal implant and screws. This was done on only on his right leg, not his left.

A few years later, Trouble began favoring his left TPLO leg and my worst nightmare came true. The local vet said it was osteoarthritis and told me to give Trouble aspirin for pain, but the specialist immediately saw a tumor at the site of the metal implant on an x-ray. Trouble had bone cancer.

A bone biopsy confirmed the osteosarcoma tumor was associated with his 2004 TPLO surgery site. Treatment for pain was amputation, which we did, but instead of chemo we added a holistic approach (massage, acupuncture, chiropractic care, Chinese herbs, nutritional supplements, home cooked diet, underwater treadmill, hydrotherapy, music, walks, and an infinite amount of love).

Trouble did well with his amputation. He was still playful, loving, and affectionate. However, a few months later he went painfully lame. An MRI revealed the cancer had metastasized to the vertebrae in his spine. At this point drugs could neither give Trouble any quality of life nor manage the pain. I was forced to let Trouble go to prevent him from suffering.

Trouble was such an angel. My heart still aches with his loss, yet I will be forever blessed for having had this precious boy in my life. Thank you, Trouble, for being no Trouble at all. I love you forever.

 *Deborah Kazsimer*

It rained into the afternoon, and they had spent most of the day in the house. When I got home, they were fractious—shoving, pushing, and growling at each other. Two sequentially knocked the phone to the floor in such short order they were scolded simultaneously, which, at least, lent some efficiency to the situation. A walk across the pasture, I decided, would perhaps dispel some of the devilment.

Boo, an old hand, ducked under the electric fence. Dyce, mindful of his size, waited for me to open the gate, as did

Zach, who didn't know where we were going. When I take all of them out freestyle, I like the choice of this pasture. Fenced with polycoated, high-tensile, electric wire, escape is unlikely, even in the event of groupthink that it would be good to hassle the neighbor's new cows.

Mz. Smith does not like the pasture, having been bit by the fence early in her tenure. Despite encouragement, she stayed in the chain link fenced yard where it is safe.

It is a special pleasure to watch Zach running across the field. The doctor who put him back together did a good job. In the last couple of days, I can already see his movement getting stronger and smoother. He must have been beautiful in his prime.

Boo must have been zapped on his way into the pasture because, upon returning, he bobbled at his favorite corner to slide under the fence, doing a couple of quick forward and backward steps. He decided not to risk it, so we all chose the gate.

Mz. Smith came out of the chain link fenced yard to give us a welcome back dance. Then Zach was struck with an independent thought to go visit the horses in the next pasture. He dove into the gap between the gate and the fence post, but Zach is a big boy, and the gate could only yield as far as the play of the chain. So Zach was stuck at his ribs, bellowing his distress at this appalling trick, while I hurried to free him. It might be cruel to say so, but it was laugh-at-the-dog funny.

Zach is such a good boy, and I can't think why he has not been adopted yet. He likes to be close and is contentedly chewing a toy behind my chair now. He is so much happier than in the kennel. He is totally housetrained (okay, I did have to remind him the walls are not his to mark, but it was only a couple drops), and he knows "down," "sit," and "come." This morning, during the passing out of the pig ears, he sat with the rest of the congregation and waited his turn like a gentleman (which is more than can be said for Wicked Smith, who is neither a gentleman nor lady and hates to wait her turn).

And thus is a slice of life in a foster home.

 *Arden Gale*

The Devine Star

In Judiasm a "beshert" can be thought of as a soul mate. It is the concept of finding the one you are divined to be with. Effie is *our* beshert. She has touched our hearts in a way I thought not possible.

As our beloved German Shepherd, Sergei, was losing his battle with cancer, Effie (whom we had not yet even heard of) was sitting on a street corner, waiting for *someone*. Sergei's passing was about the most painful experience I'd had in life; he had moved to Philadelphia with us, and I felt alone and depressed in a strange place without him.

Sergei, my baby of nine years, inspired me to become active in German Shepherd Dog rescue, so, of course, we decided to adopt our next furry companion, too. I surfed Petfinder.com and found a beautiful dog 50 miles away. She had no name, just a cage number (F-8). We saw her luminous face behind bars and a spark ignited like a shooting star. I felt empty no more.

We learned that the dog had been sitting on a corner for a whole week. Some folks had tried to catch her, but she ran away several times before they were successful. Nobody knows how she ended up on that corner, but we just say she was waiting there for us. We decided that "Effie Bahnhof" suited her perfectly. After all, "effie" means star, and "bahnhof" mean stop or station.

The day we picked up Effie, she was so scared that we had to carry her into the car. Once home she immediately went to her bed and slept. Still reeling from loss, I sat alone crying, when all of a sudden I felt something on my toes... Effie's tongue. She came from out of nowhere to kiss my toes! I laughed for the first time in days, and at that moment I realized, although we had both been abandoned, we were lucky enough to find a friend to help us heal.

That spring Effie blossomed into a happy-go-lucky girl, who makes it impossible to *ever* be sad. Whether she sits with her paws crossed in front of TV, sings to us, or begs for a Pup-A-Roni, my best friend always puts a smile on my face.

 *Monica & Larry Johnson*

Shepherd Shorts

A Georgia PEEch: My husband thought our terrier-mix, Martin, needed a buddy after Zia died. We applied with the German Shepherd Dog Rescue Group of Georgia, were approved, and after some time received a call about a four-month-old, female puppy, who had been rescued from a shelter. We all went to meet her and knew she was the one when Martin peed on her head, and she didn't mind! After adopting sweet, friendly Maya, I only regretted not having had the opportunity to see her as a young pup. But one day, as I was going back through old emails, I came across a photo of German Shepherd Dogs from the local shelter. Believe it or not, there was my unmistakable little devil (her paperwork gave her birthday as 06/06/06) as a teeny puppy in the shelter! *-Amy Rappaport*

My Girl's a BOY! I was approved as a *bone*-a-fide dog mom by my local rescue, and confident I'd be taking home a particular female, I'd painted a room pink for her and purchased doggy nail polish. Upon finally meeting "my girl," the rescue director cautioned me about her extreme dominance and need for discipline, which was not my forte by any means. Still stubborn and hopeful, I walked her until she quickly proved our mismatch by dragging me across the yard. Begrudgingly I moved on to meet several "less dominant" dogs, and to my surprise "the one" turned out to be Jackson (now Beau), a male with striking hazel eyes, who adopted me the moment we met. The pink doggy room is now used for storage, the nail polish was given away, and Beau is an absolute dream companion. *-Lisa Hall*

One Step at a Time

With Buddy being sick with cancer, we weren't looking for a big challenge, but Jake's story seemed straightforward. The website said he was five years old (he turned out to be only 2½) and that he had been turned into our local humane society when his original owner had died. He was heartworm positive, had a chronic ear infection, and by the time we found him, he had been in foster care for about six months.

It was almost Christmas when we put in our application, but the rescue volunteer understood our need to adopt while

Buddy was still fairly strong. She expedited the process, including coming to our home for the usual inspection. She saw that we have a large yard with a sturdy, six-foot fence (Jake was not our first German Shepherd), and she met both of our other dogs, Greta and Buddy.

Buddy was losing ground, and when it came time to drive the 90 miles to Montgomery, we decided to let him rest at home while we took Greta on her first-ever car trip without him. When we got to the foster home, Greta was a little intimidated by the large dogs who greeted us.

We met several dogs that day to have other options if Jake wasn't the right one. Since German Shepherds are rarely gregarious toward new people, we didn't expect him to greet us with any particular eagerness. But we were satisfied that he allowed us to walk him up and down the street with Greta nearby.

After signing the paperwork and writing the check, we headed for the car. On the way home, Jake rode quietly in the backseat with his head in my husband's lap. Greta rode in the front passenger seat next to me. No longer fearful, she was excited and curious.

At our house there were no problems between Jake and Buddy, but after exploring the house thoroughly, Jake seemed unable to settle down. We had bought him a large crate with soft padding, and I was able to lure him in with a treat. I didn't shut the door. I just wanted him to know that this was his safe place.

For the next couple hours we watched as he paced around. He would lie in the crate for a few minutes, but then he would get up and begin pacing again. Finally he went to sleep in the crate, but it was several days before he would lie near us while we watched TV.

For a few weeks, we shut Jake in the crate at night and for short periods during the day if we had to leave the house. He really didn't seem to mind, but in less than a month, we felt comfortable giving him the same freedom enjoyed by our other two dogs. At some point he even started sleeping on the couch after we went to bed at night.

Though Jake and Buddy's time together was short, I think it helped Jake get off to a good start. Buddy accepted Jake without any sign of jealousy, but he also made it clear to Jake that bullying would not be tolerated. For example, Jake saw fetch as an opportunity to chase and tackle, and Buddy did his best to curb that behavior with gentle but firm body language.

My husband, Dennis, was worried that Buddy would be possessive about his many beloved stuffed animals which he always carried around. Surprisingly, Buddy didn't seem to mind Jake picking up his toys, and Jake only picked them up curiously (never destroying them), as if he wasn't sure what their attraction was.

Buddy died exactly three weeks after we got Jake, and we sometimes reflect on the fact that Buddy and Jake probably would have been fast friends if Buddy had been healthy. This seems ironic because if Buddy hadn't been sick, Jake would not have come into our lives.

Jake has kept me very busy. When we started obedience it was clear he had some training in his first life, but he was very suspicious of strangers, and socialization became our primary motivation. At the end of his third six-week class, Jake passed the Canine Good Citizen test on the first try. We kept up with classes to continue improving Jake's demeanor around strangers, and after about six months, we cut back obedience to once a week so that we could start agility. Jake seems to enjoy agility, though I think his real aptitude might be in tracking, which we haven't yet had the opportunity to try.

After a year, Jake still struggles with home visitors. When my sister recently spent the night, Jake alternated between barking and wary alertness. After she left, it was several days before he would even enter the room in which she slept. This represents only minimal progress from the hiding he did when we first got him. While we initially thought this behavior was due to having been in multiple foster homes, I am beginning to think Jake's original owner was a hermit, which may have aggravated what is a natural tendency in German Shepherds.

We continue to work with Jake on socialization, and he happily spends his days going for walks and playing with Greta. Jake still tackles Greta when we try to play ball, so I take them into the backyard separately for this activity. "Fetch" to Jake involves chases the ball once and then playing a solo game of either running with the ball in his mouth or batting it around on the ground. Jake and Greta wrestle and play fight, usually resulting in Greta having a serious case of "wet head" from Jake's mouth, while he comes away totally dry. In the evening they both lie in bed with me while I read. Jake loves to be petted and brushed, and now that we've finally conquered his ear infection, he especially loves having his ears rubbed.

While our first German Shepherd Dog thought she was a Golden Retriever, Jake seems to know exactly who he is. He's constantly alert, guarding our home from squirrels and UPS drivers. I am proud of the progress he has made in his first year with us and hope we can give him a long, healthy life. Jake introduced us to the special rewards associated with loving an adopted dog, and though he may be our first rescue, I am sure he won't be our last. Maybe there will even be some fosters in our future!

 *Ginger Campbell*

The Sweetheart and The Gentleman

We named our first rescued German Shepherd Dog Schatze, after our beloved Shepherd, Sweetheart. (*Schatze* means "sweetheart" in German). Schatze was six months old and had been surrendered with her siblings when we adopted her from German Shepherd Dog Rescue Group of Georgia (GSDRGA). We weathered her puppyhood well, she trained easily, and we even became friends with her foster parents, Susan and Jim. They visited a few times with their German Shepherd, Zoey, and whomever they were fostering at the time. On one occasion they brought along an adult male foster dog with such a beautiful black coat they were compelled to name him Cole.

Cole was a gentle giant who played nicely with Schatze and Zoey. He was easy to fall in love with, and when he looked up at me with loving brown eyes and put his huge head on my lap, I knew he would be a great addition to our home. This poor guy had been in a shelter for four months after being on the road for a long time. He was heartworm positive when rescued and had scabs all over his body from insect bites. GSDRGA treated him for heartworm, and in spite of his hardships, he remained calm, friendly, and stoic. He was a true "gentleman."

My husband, Mickey, and I agreed that we would love to have Cole as part of our family, but unfortunately Cole was already slated for a new home the next day. While we wanted Cole to be happy, we couldn't help wishing that maybe it wouldn't work.

The following day Jim and Susan took Cole to his potential new home, and all went quite well...at first. Somehow Cole, the quiet gentleman, ended up with the family's prized cat's head in his mouth! Nobody was sure if he didn't like the cat or just wanted to play, nor did they take the time to find out. Jim, Susan, and Cole were promptly escorted through the door.

Susan called when they returned home with Cole and said that he was still available for adoption. Our hearts soared, and we told Susan we would take him. We had already been cleared for adoption since we had adopted Schatze from GSDRGA, so we picked him up and added him to our pack right away.

Schatze and Cole became fast friends. They romp together and can be found lying side-by-side in companionship. Sometimes I feel like the Pied Piper with two, one-hundred-pound German Shepherds following behind. They make a great pair—playful together but calm around our guests when we have friends in for dinner. In the evenings my husband sits on the floor between Schatze and Cole, throwing balls to Schatze and petting Cole's head on his lap. In the morning we are awakened with love licks from our babies, our constant source of affection.

Schatze and Cole, our sweetheart and gentleman, make our family and lives complete.

 *Vicki Rosenbaum*

What a Tripp!

First, let me say this: Driving from Shelby County, Alabama, to New Hampshire and back in 60 hours was a wonderful experience. We had a vanload of dogs on the way there, and on the way back, well, we were supposed to be empty.

Kristi and I are filling up the tank in Virginia when a man runs up to me, saying, "What is it that y'all do?" I start to tell him, but he interrupts: "I have this dog, a German Shepherd that I have to find a home for or take him to get fried." Those are the words he uses: "Get fried." I'm assuming he means to take him to a shelter to be euthanized, but all I really hear is "German Shepherd" and "fried," and now I am thinking, "Oh no, how weird is this? Does he know I do German Shepherd rescue? This would only happen to *me*."

So I ask the details about the dog, and of course, he's not neutered but he is young, purebred, and healthy. Of course, he's wonderful: good with kids, cats, children, housetrained, etc. Of course, the urgency is because the man has started a new job where he is on call 24/7 as a maintenance man, so he doesn't have time to work with the dog. And of course, the dog barks, disturbing the neighbors who then call the police, and the owner will get fined if there is one more occurrence.

I say to him, "Well, I happen to do German Shepherd rescue. I'll need to see your dog."

The guys says, "Oh, no problem. I just live down the road. I'll go get him."

By this time Kristi has pumped the gas and is walking over with a puzzled and perplexed look on her face. I fill Kristi in and call GSRCA's president to ask what to do. She says, "Well, this is what rescue is all about. Go ahead and take the dog, and we'll find somewhere to put him."

The man returns with the dog, who immediately hops right into an empty crate in the van and doesn't make as much as a peep on the way back to Alabama. Devising a name for him doesn't take long as "Tripp" is just so obvious. Kristi says, "And *what* is wrong with this dog?" He seems to be a model canine citizen.

It's very late Sunday night when we finally make it to my house. The minutes that pass as we fumble to put together my brand new "emergency crate" for Tripp are grueling because we're so tired. We finish, Tripp gets a potty break, and then he's in his crate. But the night is not to be restful because as soon as Kristi leaves, it begins...the barking.

It's the most ear-piercing bark I have ever heard, and it goes on and on. I stupidly lean over his crate and he aims one directly into my ear. My ear rings for days, and I still think I lost a bit of hearing from it. Wow! So this is why the owner got a citation for disturbing the peace.

We don't have room to foster Tripp in my house, so we ask one of our local foster homes to take him. I, umm, forget, umm, to tell David about Tripp's special talent, and David calls me first thing the next morning. "Tripp can't stay at my house or my wife will divorce me," he says. It seems Tripp started barking in the middle of the night and wouldn't hush, so David had to drive him around in the car like you'd do for a baby. David says to me, "He has the loudest bark I have ever heard." Oh, does he?

So I trade Tripp with David for my foster, Vito. Ahh...nice, quiet Vito. I'm back to the barking until we realize that Tripp's big problem is with crating and loneliness. We gradually introduce him to our dogs, Trinka and Scooby, and they all get along. Scooby is actually thrilled to have another boy his size to play with, and the barking ceases to be an issue. Before long, Tripp is surprisingly ready for a new home.

The side of our van says, *"Going the Distance to Save Lives,"* and that's just what we did on our way home from New Hampshire. Like the GSRCA president said, it's what rescue is all about.

 *Chris Wilson*

Clever and the Clown

Xena and Gabby were "saved" from the dangerous streets of Paterson, NJ, and taken to a local shelter. Right before they were to be euthanized, Garden State German Shepherd Rescue (GSGSR) pulled them from the shelter and put them in boarding. That's where they stayed for a few months until I was asked to take them to the vet for spaying. My instructions were to return them to where they were boarded, but after seeing these sweet girls jump up on people and finding out they weren't housebroken, I thought they would have a better chance of finding a forever home if I could teach them proper "petiquette."

Xena and Gabby were sweet, cute, and *inseparable*, so they would have to be adopted together. Xena (the smarter of the two) caught on to housebreaking in about a week, but Gabby took quite a bit longer. Once they figured out pottying outside, they would go out the door, spin around, face the door, and pee and poop right on the doormat! (At least it made for easy clean up.) My Roxy always gave them a strange look as she passed by them on her way off the deck and into the yard to do her business.

Within a month both Xena and Gabby were housebroken and could sit on command. Xena could go from a "sit" to a "down" and give her paw. Gabby did not catch on to down and paw, mainly because she was too busy dancing around in circles, anticipating cookies, to concentrate on her lessons.

Whenever Roxy and "Gabby the Clown" would try to play, "Xena the Fun Police" would put herself in between them. When everyone was acceptably calm, Xena would go lay down. This process went on, day after day, until eventually, with a little help from me, Xena let go enough to allow Gabby and Roxy to have a good time. Xena would never play with them, instead preferring to watch from the sidelines like an overprotective mom.

One day we set up a meet and greet for Xena and Gabby at a local dog park with a potential adopter named Cathy. Cathy brought several friends and family members to meet the girls, and while Gabby and Roxy ran off to play, Xena stayed behind with the people. When an obnoxious dog kept jumping on Cathy's nephew, Xena immediately put herself between the dog and the boy, letting the other dog know she meant business. It was then that I knew the girls had found their new family. Xena and Gabby now live as beloved family pets in a beautiful house with a big yard. They go on frequent road trips with Cathy, and after some additional training, they have become model canine citizens.

 *Lisa Lombardo*

Odd Man Out

I t was three years ago when Brutus came into my life. Two months before I had lost my gorgeous, black and tan German Shepherd Dog, Baron—my best friend for eleven years. I was so devastated by his loss that I couldn't consider getting another dog who even resembled him, so when I saw Brutus on the German Shepherd website and read his sweet story, I knew he was perfect for me.

You're probably wondering what I mean. See, Brutus had been at the Birmingham Humane Society for some time. They didn't euthanize him because he was such a sweet boy, but still nobody would adopt him. As an extra-large, black dog with huge feet and "soft" ears, he just didn't fit the description of a "proper" German Shepherd.

Thank goodness a foster family became available with a private German Shepherd rescue. Brutus went to live with them and was placed on the rescue's website. True to form, he was not adopted. Everyone who applied for a German Shepherd wanted a dog who looked like a German Shepherd, but Brutus was the perfect dog for me.

Brutus brought the joy to my life that I so desperately needed. Every day I laugh at his goofy antics, and I love taking pictures of him. His ears have their own special style, which goes perfectly with his personality and makes for great photos. Poor muscle tone from being in runs all his life used to keep him falling all over his big feet and doing somersaults, which was a little sad but terribly funny. And though he's stronger and manages himself better now, he still always keeps me laughing.

Thank you, everyone, for not adopting Brutus and saving the best "best friend" for me!

 *Jean Henderson*

A Tale of Two Tails

I t happened so quickly. One day he was fine, the next day he was coughing a little; then his breathing became labored and loud. Trooper was getting worse, and the vet explained that there was nothing more he could do. I held Trooper gently and whispered that it was okay for him to go, and he relaxed and heaved his last breath. Trooper the Magnificent, the oversized, purebred German Shepherd with the huge feet and beautiful eyes, had been vanquished by aspiration pneumonia—just like that.

We had lost our other German Shepherd, Greta the Braveheart, just a few short years earlier. Despite a host of medical issues too long to list, her indomitable spirit never wavered. Her courage and faithfulness was an inspiration.

Suddenly we were a family without a dog, and the unused dog bowls and dog beds were sad reminders of happier days. Although we had jokingly complained that our job was to "let the dogs in, let the dogs out," and we certainly didn't miss the tumbleweeds of dog hair constantly wafting about the house, we had to admit it: the loneliness of life without a dog was filling our hearts.

Even so, we had agreed to wait at least a year before getting another canine companion. We thought of the places we could travel, without worrying that furry friends had been left behind. We thought of the money saved in upkeep. I confess I liked how clean the house stayed. Life was simpler, but it was missing something.

Then the unexpected happened. My husband, Mark, saw the picture in the local paper. He mentioned it at dinner that evening—Bill, a beautiful male German Shepherd with incredibly sad eyes and floppy ears, needed a home...again. Thrice the victim of a broken home, Bill had been available for a while, but no one had expressed interest. I said, "How sad, but please don't show me that picture. You know what will happen if you show me that picture." After pulling the paper out of the recycling bin and rustling through the pages, Mark carefully folded the paper and set Bill's beautiful face before me on the dinner table. I cried.

Bill looked hauntingly like Trooper—same classic black and tan German Shepherd markings, same gorgeous, brown eyes, same huge frame—and those endearing floppy ears! The story explained Bill's predicament, that he was the collateral damage from a breakup; no one could keep a large dog in their new situations, and Bill was getting visibly more depressed with each day. That clinched it; we were going to adopt Bill.

But it didn't end there. I went online to the rescue website to fill out the paperwork, and that's when I saw her. At first I did a double-take, as I thought I was looking at a picture of our Greta—same dark markings, same regal pose, same indomitable spirit in those eyes. My heartstrings quivered, and I knew I also wanted to give this dog, Niki, a home.

Obviously a purebred German Shepherd, Niki was found as a stray and then placed in a shelter. Every effort had been made to find her owners to no avail, and time was running out. The staff was heartbroken that Niki was scheduled for euthanasia, and in desperation at the last hour, they called German Shepherd rescue. A rescue volunteer jumped into her vehicle, made the long drive to the desert town, and picked up Niki—just in time. Then something remarkable happened, something she had never seen before. As they were walking to the car, Niki bolted back to the shelter and gave each worker a kiss on the hand. It's as if she knew they had loved her and saved her life. She was saying "Thank you, and goodbye."

We adopted Bill and Niki on the same day (which happened to be Mother's Day) at a rescue event. They had never met each other but quickly adapted to life together as part of the Thompson pack. Now we're back to long walks, Frisbee, and the gratification of mutual respect and affection.

New tumbleweeds of dog hair fill our halls, but we see them as happy hallmarks of a life lived with dogs.

German Shepherd Dogs—noble sentinels, guardians, companions, and friends—would without hesitation lay down their lives to protect us. It must be so hard for them to lose their owners because they are animals of such courage and loyalty. How can they possibly comprehend the shortcomings of the humans they unquestioningly love and protect? I look at our two new canine family members, and I often wonder about their "other" people. Do the dogs remember them? Miss them? Worry about them? Knowing German Shepherds, they do.

 *Anne Thompson*

Dream Big

My dog and I met because of a dream. It was late November or early December, and I was giggling and talking in my sleep. In the dream my dog, Baxter, was licking my face and I was so happy—until I awoke to the disappointment that there was no "Baxter" ready to greet me. I thought perhaps I was missing something in my life; perhaps I needed a dog.

I began my search, but it proved to be more difficult than expected, until I went to the Big Shanty festival in downtown Kennesaw, GA. There I found an adoption booth and was told they did have one dog, as they pointed to the back of the booth. He was scrawny and wearing headgear from a recent surgery, sporting a dreadful pin in his leg. My first thought was, "Seriously? Are you kidding me?" He came over to me on shaky legs, desperately dragging that back one. He rested his head in the palm of my hand, looked up at me the way only a dog could, and I found myself asking the woman behind the booth, "Does he have a name?"

She smiled at me and said, "Yes, we call him Baxter." I was stunned speechless, recalling the dream just months earlier. I then asked, "How old is he?" and to that she replied, "We're not sure, but we estimate he was born in late November, early December." My friend and I looked at each other in disbelief because we both knew exactly when I had had my dream. Of course, the next part was easy. Out came the paperwork and Baxter officially became mine—my first dog, a 20-pound German Shepherd pup.

I suppose it was about a year later when I took Baxter out for his early morning piddle, and I was sporting pajamas and bed-head hair, yawning, still half asleep at 6:00am, trying to be patient as Baxter chose his spot. Suddenly, the force of Baxter leaping over a large bush swung me around, and what I saw next were two very large hands in front of my face. Baxter never hesitated. He lunged, knocked the guy down, and went for his throat. I'd never seen this side of my dog before. The guy carefully got to his feet, not making any sudden movements, crept to the other side of the street and walked slowly away, not looking in our direction, not saying a word. Meanwhile, Baxter was pulling, lunging, and trying to get free, so he could chase the man.

Shaking terribly and barely able to stand on my rubbery legs, I finally got Baxter inside the house. Naturally I phoned the police and then my mom, who reminded me that I would have been out there with a small dog had I gone with my original intent. Thank goodness Baxter found me instead. He saved me, and I owe him a great deal for that.

Recently, while spending a Sunday meandering in downtown Kennesaw and enjoying some pre-fall weather, I came across one of my favorite haunts, The Painted Butterfly. It's owned by my dear friend, Holly Jones-Buttimer, who has a unique way of capturing life on canvas, whether it's an enchanted butterfly or the heart and soul of someone's treasured pet. Her dog, Elvis, a harlequin Great Dane, is every bit his namesake, and we were discussing a painting that looked like him when Holly showed me another portrait— this one of a German Shepherd. I loved it, of course, and so I shared with her the story of how Baxter and I came to be best friends and housemates. She loved the story and told me she'd like to paint him. Incredibly honored, I made arrangements to bring Baxter to her shop.

When the painting was completed, Holly shared with me that, before she began the painting, she wasn't sure what she was going to choose as the canvas. People often bring her trash, recycled items that she turns into treasure, so for Baxter's portrait she ultimately chose an old window someone had dropped off. She painted his picture on the front and then turned it around to paint the back, only to find that someone had written the words, "DREAM BIG," on the window glass. She was surprised at her find, but I wasn't; since Baxter came into my life after the dream I'd had, it only seemed fitting that those words be a part of the painting honoring him.

It's strange to think that a dream would lead me to a dog who would save my life and become the inspiration for a portrait. I have the perfect spot picked out for it, right above the top of the stairs where Baxter normally rests each night, guarding me as I sleep. Good boy, Baxter!

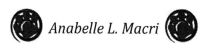 *Anabelle L. Macri*

Father's Day Friend

When illness forced us to put our beloved German Shepherd to sleep, my husband, James, was devastated. I decided a new puppy would be the perfect Father's Day gift to bring some sunshine back into his life. A co-worker informed me about Greater California German Shepherd Rescue (GCGSR), and I began visiting their website daily, hoping for the perfect pup.

We had our hearts set on a puppy until I came across Jaxon, who was a little older. He was beautiful—just the right color we were looking for—and James and I immediately fell in love with Jaxon's picture.

James went to see the GCGSR rescue dogs at a Petsmart adoption day in Rancho Cordova that weekend, but unfortunately he was told that Jaxon would not be there until the following weekend. James worried all week that Jaxon would be adopted by then, but he went back to the next adoption day anyway. He was walking through the store as the dogs were brought in, and as soon as he saw Jaxon, he knew it was him. What's more, Jaxon immediately went to James as though he'd come for the sole purpose of meeting him. At that moment, my husband knew Jaxon was the dog for us.

Jaxon is now a playful 2½-year-old who has come a long way from when we got him. He has a very proud gait, which we love to watch, he is great with our grandkids, and we could not have found a more loving dog. To imagine someone thought he would not be a good family pet! Jaxon turned out to not just be a great Father's Day present for James—our rescued dog's warm, loving presence is truly a gift for our entire family.

 *Estelle & James Jones*

Not Housebroken
Doesn't Mean Broken

Nigel and Nicky's mom and dad (both White German Shepherd Dogs) ended up in a shelter in Oklahoma as a result of their breeder quitting the trade. Both would have been put to sleep if "OK Save-A-Dog" (aka "K9Savers") hadn't pulled them out in time. On that day the rescuers had no idea that they hadn't just saved two lives...

They had actually saved nine! About two weeks after the dogs were taken from the shelter, momma gave birth to five girls and two boys. I had recently lost three White German

Shepherd Dogs to cancer in close succession, so I adopted both boys. I live in Southwest Texas, but since I have many rescue contacts from being involved with rescue for years, I was able to set up a transport and get them within two-and-a-half hours driving distance from me.

Nigel and Nicky (as I named them) were as cute as could be, but they took extra long to housebreak because of illnesses resulting in diarrhea, bloody stool, and many vet visits. They were tested for everything but came up negative, so the vets didn't know how to help them. The decision was made to explore the idea that the symptoms could be from food allergies, and with that we were finally on the road to recovery. "Top of the line" foods turned out *not* to be the answer—what we needed was food with a few, simple ingredients.

Nigel is much smaller than his brother, Nicky, and he still seems like a puppy at over two years old. He even still has a puppy bark. His small size makes him my "Snuggie Bunny." He's the perfect size for a cuddle, and he loves it.

Some people may not have put up with the housebreaking issue and would have thrown Nigel and Nicky outside for life (or worse), but for me they were just what the doctor ordered. These two boys are the loves of my life, and I am thankful every day for adopting them.

 *Annmarie Mikelski*

Shepherd Shorts

Class Clown Settles Down: Mitchell was the cutest German Shepherd puppy, with a scarf and a floppy ear. On the 3½ hour drive home after adopting him, we thought he would sit between my son and me in the backseat. Instead he decided to lie across both of our laps *the whole time*! When it came time to put him in obedience class, I was sure that, being a German Shepherd, he would be the star pupil. But again, Mitchell had other plans. He was the star, all right, but it was as the class clown. Of course, as he matured, Mitchell settled down, and in addition to laughter and entertainment, he now provides us with sympathy, joy, and love.
-Kandra Miller

Multilingual Mystique: When we adopted Mystique she was hesitant, shy, and afraid of *everything*, but that didn't last long. In no time she became our other dog's best friend, our cat's snuggle buddy, and our lap-warmer. What's more, in German, English, *and* Sign Language she understands: come, sit, stay, and lay down. She fetches her ball and drops it on command, and she "gives me five" with alternating paws. But after six months with Mystique, there is still one mystery: How could someone throw away such a wonderful dog? Well you know what they say: *"Dem Einen sein Stall ist dem anderen sein Königreich"* (similar to "one man's trash is another man's treasure"). Mystique is surely our treasure! *-Pam Martinez*

Turkish Delight

German Shepherd Rescue of Central Alabama (GSRCA) pulled a year-old male German Shepherd Dog from a large suburban shelter. He was typical of many of the rescues taken into GSRCA—malnourished, sick, and generally neglected.

Evidently someone had not been kind to him. Quick movements or any loud noise would have him dropping into a submissive belly crawl, as if ready to accept punishment. He was insecure and fearful and had the disturbing dietary hygiene issue of eating his own feces and urine.

But the most tragic issues were the orthopedic ones. He could walk, but trotting or running turned into bunny-hops. He flailed around a lot and seemed uncomfortable. X-rays showed he had probably been hit by a car at an early age, badly damaging both hips which had healed incorrectly. Immediate euthanasia was advised.

Instead, GSRCA named him Turke (a tough guy name which means "headstrong") and got him a second opinion from an orthopedic specialist. This vet felt he was a good candidate for *femoral head osteotomy* (FHO), which meant removing the femoral heads from both hips and letting the ligaments and tendons become the supporting structure.

I'm a volunteer for GSRCA and helped pull Turke from the shelter that September. I transported him to all the vet clinics and fostered him for nine months. Although I always wanted him to find a loving, forever home, I was often dismayed when potential adopters called to discuss him. The discussion and concerns always came around to their apprehension of adopting a dog with "hip issues." How could I get across to people that his personality and companionship far outweighed any potential arthritic hip problems? I couldn't, so I ended up adopting him myself.

Turke is now strong and large, and he often acts like a clown. He's a confident guardian in his home but so gentle that children can hug him and even play with his ears and teeth. A tall boy with a big heart and intelligent eyes, Turke is the happiest dog we have ever known. And although he is a grown-up dog, he can tumble with the best of the young ones, run like the wind, and play chase, fetch, and catch. Naturally he's spoiled and has become fairly snobby and selective with his food choices (which no longer include his own waste).

Except for the missing toes and slightly cow-hocked rear legs you wouldn't know Turke had been rolled under a vehicle as a puppy, healed incorrectly, and spent months crippled. You can barely see the long incisions down each hip and leg where the orthopedic surgeon removed the femoral heads to correctly align his hips. In fact, there's very little resemblance to the insecure, scrawny rat we first met. Like so many rescued dogs, Turke had a massive transformation.

The biggest remaining problem for Turke is his "miss-pees." Because the hip surgery didn't allow for proper hind leg lifting, Turke always manages to urinate on his front legs and even hit his face if he looks down. It's just part of his comedy, but everything else is just fine.

Turke has beaten the Reaper at least three times, and we thank everyone along the way who helped him. As a direct result of their kindness, the one who seemed like a lost cause has become one of my best friends—our life together is sweeter than a Turkish Delight!

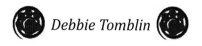 *Debbie Tomblin*

The Quarterback

Early last year my family decided it was time to add another member to our ranks, so we eagerly set out to adopt a dog. We weren't particular about a puppy or an older dog—we just wanted a dog who needed us as much as we needed him (or her). While searching the internet for possibilities, I stumbled across a courtesy listing for an adorable German Shepherd puppy named Frisco from a local rescue group. I wasn't quite ready at that time, even though I thought he was the perfect pup. I tried to put him out of my head because I was sure that by the time we were ready to bring someone home, he'd be gone.

A few weeks went by, and we were still looking. Again I stumbled onto Frisco's listing, so I called to arrange a meeting. That afternoon, I stopped by his foster home with two of our children in tow, and we all immediately fell in love—Frisco was perfect in every way.

It turns out Frisco and his littermates had quite a rough start. A farmer had trapped their feral mom and took her, along with her puppies, to a shelter. Because they were given only 72 hours to find homes before they'd be euthanized, Coastal White German Shepherd Dog Rescue stepped in and put the family into one of their foster homes. Though the pups had wonderful temperaments, their mom was extremely aggressive toward humans and viciously attacked the foster mom several times (with one attack almost resulting in a hospital trip). Despite the foster family's best efforts, the mom had to be put down because she was a danger to people, and the pups ended up with very bad pneumonia. The vets were not even sure if Frisco would make it, but he was a fighter and pulled through. By the time my family met Frisco, he was one of only two pups still looking for a home. We scheduled the requisite home inspection for the very next day.

Frisco and his littermate arrived at our house and tentatively took a look around. Soon they were running in the yard and having a good time. It took a few minutes, but Frisco came to me and enjoyed some pets and rubs. Then we took him inside to see how he would react to our adopted cat. He didn't mind at all, and in fact, when it was time for Frisco to leave, he wouldn't! He wrapped himself around my legs and refused to move. It was the beginning of a true "love affair."

When shortly after the visit we heard we were approved to adopt Frisco, we immediately went to pick him up, only stopping at the store for supplies along the way. We re-christened him Halen, and he's been a joy to us every day since. We have three children (ages seven, five, and two), and he is attentive to each of their needs. He spends his time snuggling with the older two and serves as quarterback for the two-year-old, who likes to "play" tackle football with him. Halen manages to make a dog lover out of anyone, and we can't imagine our lives without him.

 *Tara Marie Kully*

Beauty and the Bimmer

B eauty is a four-year-old, classic German Shepherd who has a guardian angel watching over her. When she was found, she was weak, emaciated, and suffering from an injury to her leg. Her rescuer took Beauty in, had her treated by a veterinarian, and helped her gain some much needed weight. The vet noted that she has a prior injury to her hind leg, causing her to walk with a slight limp. So Beauty will most likely require medication for arthritis as she gets older, but who won't?

I was volunteering to help train Beauty when Roger, the dog trainer, looked at me in class one day and, pointing to Beauty, said, "She is a special dog."

"Hmm," I thought, "what does he mean by that?" At that time all I knew about her was to be careful around other dogs, especially small ones. Beauty had a little hitch in her get along and snarled at dogs when they came too close.

I began walking her four times a week to reinforce the training classes, and sure enough it started to pay off. As we walked down the street, her nose would nuzzle my left hand as if to say, "Thank you for taking me out today. I get so bored in that kennel." I would always bring her a treat, and we'd sit on the grass at the halfway point under the palm trees. We would practice all her commands, and she'd never miss a beat, always wanting to please.

We started to form a strong bond. I couldn't wait to get to the kennel after work so I could walk her. Lynn, Kathy, or Desi would bring her out to me, and Beauty would always be excited to go. "Heel, Beauty," and off we went.

Months went by and Beauty was really improving around other dogs. I could now walk her within inches of them without her barking or snarling. She was behaving *beautifully*.

I could never understand why no one ever took an interest in her. The months went by, and lots of other dogs were adopted but not Beauty. I knew she needed a special family that could handle her, and there were several people interested at adoption events but never a strong lead. "Don't worry, Beauty," I'd tell her as we walked along, "your family is looking for you, and they just don't know where you are yet."

And then I received an email from one of our adoption counselors. There was a man interested in Beauty. He had just lost his 20-year-old son. "How very sad," I thought and wondered if now was a good time for him to adopt a dog. Then I didn't hear anything more about him and read on the volunteer blog several days later that Beauty's lead had fizzled. "I guess they weren't the right ones, girl."

But the next week brought another email about Beauty. The man, John, decided to come take a look after all. His wife wasn't ready, but the rest of the family was now on board.

The day before the meeting, I bathed her and brushed her out. "You are beautiful," I told her, and we went on our last walk together. The next day I arrived early for our meeting, so I could brush her out once again. John drove up from San Diego in a BMW (Bimmer) convertible. I thought, "How is he going to transport a German Shepherd in a convertible? I guess he won't be taking her today." He climbed out of his car and stared at Beauty with a huge smile on his face. "He likes her," I thought, as I proudly showed him how well she knew her commands. It was obviously a love connection, and John was ready to take her home. He told me the loss of his son was especially hard on his younger son. They were only a few years apart, and it was important for Beauty and his son to bond. "Whoever walks Beauty will bond with Beauty," I said.

We went through the necessary paperwork, and then it was time to say goodbye. At that moment all I felt was joy for my favorite rescue as she hopped into the back of his Bimmer. As they drove off, she turned her head to look at me, and I stared at her until she was out of sight. Three weeks later I emailed John to check in. Beauty was doing great. "She gets three walks a day. I walk her in the morning, my wife walks her midday, and my son walks her after school."

It was truly a fairytale ending for my Beauty. Though it may have taken a while for her perfect family to come along, it was well worth the wait.

 *Lois Conlon*

Pick of the Litter

My husband and I received a phone call about a year after we bought our female German Shepherd, Shelby. It was the lady who sold her to us, wanting to know if we would take Shelby's brother, Rommell. He had been the pick of the litter, but his owner no longer had time for him and wanted to get rid of him.

My husband and I did not hesitate, and he immediately made the almost three-hour drive to pick up Rommell (now Roman). I was not prepared for what I saw when the boys arrived back home together. My new baby was a terrified, dirty, pitiful bag of bones who was too scared to get out of the truck. I begged and coaxed with treats for over an hour—even enlisting the help of my parents—to no avail. My husband finally had to crawl into the backseat and lift Roman out, so we could carry him into the house.

Apparently Roman's living conditions had been deplorable. He was sleeping in the dirt underneath a house and eating whatever scraps were put in the food bowl he shared with other animals. At a year and a half, he weighed only 45 pounds, while his sister was weighing in at a healthy 65 pounds. He was severely malnourished and covered in fleas, with his hair falling out. All we could do was give him a bath, fix him a big bowl of food, and hope we could help him to recover.

The next day we went to the vet and updated him on his shots (not surprisingly, his owner never kept any medical records). We introduced him to his blood sister, Shelby, and his other new "sister," Lexi, an Australian Cattle dog, who also came from horrible conditions. They have all been inseparable ever since, and now he has another new Black Lab/Australian Shepherd-mix "brother," Kilo.

Roman has taken well to his new indoor life. He is a happy, clean, 80-pound boy, who talks a lot and is very protective of his momma (with whom he likes to snuggle at night). He may have originally been picked by the wrong person, but he fits into our family just right.

 *Danielle Mullen*

Shepherd Souls

Xena was destined to be a "foster failure." We had an immediate, unexplainable connection as soon as she entered my home, and I knew I wouldn't be adopting her out to anyone except me! Xena and her littermates were just four weeks old when they (along with their mother) were rescued from an animal control facility by German Shepherd Rescue of Central Alabama (GSRCA). They were all in horrid condition—weak and covered with sores—looking and smelling as if they had been born in a sewer. Because these pups were such fighters, we named them after superheroes: Xena, Thor, Karma, Storm, and Sheera. And because their mom was so docile, we named her Harmony.

As Xena grew, the thing that made her so special to me became apparent. She began to take on the looks of my heart dog, Inga von Tooten (aka Tootie), who passed away two years earlier. But there was more than just a physical similarity; Xena had a familiar sparkle in her eyes.

Tootie loved me with a deep love, and it was mutual. Born at my home and initially rejected by her mother, I constantly reminded her that she would always have a home with me. She was so smart and eager to please that she passed her CGC (Canine Good Citizen) test before she was a year old. She was a natural comedian, and things were never dull with her antics. I had wanted Tootie to become a therapy dog, but Tootie didn't share that ambition. She loved going—going with me, going for rides—but where she really loved going was home.

Then came a year to forget. My mother died unexpectedly in April, my father died unexpectedly in August, and in December, at barely five years old, Tootie apparently suffered a sudden *spinal cord infarction* (stroke), and her spinal cord itself was liquefying. I was suddenly left with only one choice. I knew it was the right thing to do, but I couldn't imagine my life without her. My only consolation was that Tootie, Mom, and Dad were all together and would see me through somehow.

The heartache has lessened over time, but it has never completely subsided. Maybe that's just how it is for people who have suddenly lost a dear soul without time to prepare. I think of Tootie often and still cry for her at times. She was one of a kind, and there would never be another dog like her...until Xena.

Xena, my angel princess, excelled in her first puppy obedience class and seems destined to become a therapy dog in record time. She loves all people, enjoys going places, and is such a social butterfly! She has the gift to brighten spirits, showing people that the German Shepherd breed is a loving and sensitive one. Though many think of them only as police dogs, dangerous guard dogs, or war heroes, Xena demonstrates that the reason German Shepherd Dogs excel in those jobs is because of their utter devotion to their handlers. That is the true core of the Shepherd.

By the age of six months, Xena was diagnosed with severe, genetic hip dysplasia. This inherent trait is one of the main reasons people should not breed their dogs without knowing the hip condition of the parents. This can only be done by x-raying hips at two years of age and having the hips graded by the OFA (Orthopedic Foundation for Animals). Fortunately I knew a wonderful vet, Dr. James Milton, who had been Tootie's vet during her illness. I reminded Dr. Milton of Tootie and told him just how much she and Xena were alike. I think he understood my feelings.

This time our prognosis was good, and Xena's problem could be fixed with surgery. Caring for her during the slow recovery period has made me feel like I was given more time with Tootie, time enough to accept what had happened and time enough to show her how much she was loved. Even though the road was rough in the beginning, we got through it together. Xena is running and playing again as if nothing ever happened, but it did—my heart found healing though her infirmity. She may or may not ever achieve the title TD (Therapy Dog), but she has already achieved the title BF (Best Friend).

Chris Wilson

Taken by Storm

My husband (then fiancé) was fresh out of law school, and we'd just gotten our first place together. I worked as a research assistant for a local firm, and he was studying for his bar exam, taking classes at night. We'd discussed adopting a dog, and although I ever-so-slightly preferred cats, with him out at night I desperately needed a walking companion for my nightly treks. We considered a German Shepherd, but I thought our two-bedroom apartment would be too small.

One day, while browsing profiles on Petfinder.com, I stumbled across a three-year-old female German Shepherd.

What caught my eye most was the fact that she was only 60 pounds. We decided to fill out her application, and within a short time our reference calls were done, and we were ready for our home visit. Storm was on her way to see us.

It was love at first sight. Storm was nervous and skinny but still overwhelmingly beautiful. She had a coat that was longer and softer than most German Shepherds, a beautiful face and build, and she greeted us with soft and plentiful kisses. We listened to her story with sorrow and awe. Storm was one of the rare rescue dogs accompanied by AKC papers. She'd been bred in Hawaii to Amos' Rusty and the oddly named Smap, and then she was purchased by a military family. They brought her with them when they were transferred from Hawaii to Maryland, but shortly thereafter they were again transferred to a place that didn't allow pets. So before she was three years old, Storm and her papers were abandoned at a local humane society.

Lucky for Storm, the fine people of Chesapeake Shepherd and K-9 Rescue (CSK-9) took interest and brought her into foster care. From there she was adopted by a retired detective who kept her only one night and then returned her because she had severe separation anxiety and was a panic pooper.

We took it all in, signed her papers without hesitation, and Storm turned out to be everything we expected (and some things we hadn't). She *was* a panic pooper with severe separation anxiety, but she was also extremely intelligent, obedient, and quick to bond. Before long we had her panic and anxiety under control, and she was learning to play Frisbee, fetch, and to tell the difference between her many toys. Storm knows four different toys by name and will bring you whichever one you ask for. She learned this within months of her adoption and happily memorizes new toys when they come into the house.

Almost a year and a half later we got married. Around that time we noticed some changes in Storm. She had trouble doing her business and sometimes had bleeding or loose stools. We'd taken her to the vet for similar problems before, and they told us that, as many German Shepherds do, she likely had irritable bowel syndrome. But this time was different, with the symptoms lasting much longer. She began licking at her backside and crying out when she tried to relieve herself. One day I lifted her tail and nearly screamed; it looked as though a bomb had gone off in her backside. The next day my husband took her straight to the vet and called me at work with news that left me in tears. Storm, our beautiful, lively girl, had a chronic and life-threatening disease called *Peri-anal Fistula* (PF). The medication she would need, quite possibly for the rest of her life, would cost us $250 per month and might take months to be effective or never be effective at all.

As underemployed newlyweds, this was hard news to take. We did a lot of soul searching and started scraping funds together. We contacted CSK-9, and when we told them what was going on, they sent us $800 to cover her current vet bills and a second opinion. I will be forever grateful for their generosity.

The second opinion confirmed her diagnosis. We were devastated, and my husband did not know how we could afford to keep her, but I think he knew that the other option involved losing me. With the help of a Yahoo forum dedicated to PF, we found tips on diet changes, topical treatments, and discounts on her prescription medication. We slowly came to terms with the fact that her disease was incurable and focused on controlling her symptoms.

After a year and a half of treatment and a limited-ingredient diet, Storm became symptom-free and has sustained her health for over a year. She is now a healthy, beautiful, 6½-year-old dog, who is often mistaken for much younger. Everywhere we go we get compliments on her beauty and wonderful personality, and she still beats every dog in the dog park to a Frisbee, even outrunning the youngsters. Moreover, we recently began fostering through Mid-Atlantic German Shepherd Rescue, and Storm has become a wonderful role model for other wayward dogs.

Storm is the heart of our family and an inspiration to any other family dealing with PF or other auto-immune disorders. She is proof that dogs like her can survive and thrive. Whether working as a "donation dog" or teaching a foster sibling to play "tug," Storm continues to be an outstanding ambassador for her breed, helping others in need through her experience and kind nature, so that they may see light at the end of the darkest tunnel, just as we did.

 *Rebecca Goldring*

Animal Magnetism

The minute I saw Leila's photo on Petfinder.com I knew she was ours. My husband questioned how I could be so sure about a picture on the computer, but I just knew in my heart she belonged with us. Like us, our 11-year-old German Shepherd Dog, Lulu, was still moping after our other German Shepherd, Emma, died suddenly. And having known Emma, she would want to share the space she left in our hearts and home with another dog who needed a better life.

By the time we learned that two-year-old Leila, whom we renamed Molly, had been found on the streets of Caddo Parish, Louisiana, and was undergoing heartworm treatment, in my mind she was already ours. She was smaller than the average German Shepherd, maybe the runt of the litter. She was skittish and uncertain. She had the traditional German Shepherd black and tan saddle coat with dark hair that covered a completely silver undercoat. In addition, she had a tiny shock of black hair that stuck up about a quarter inch out of a head of golden hair as if to say, "I'm unique."

When dropping her off, the director of the German Shepherd Rescue assured Molly that she would like it in her new home, but Molly clearly wasn't so sure. However, once Lulu jumped on the bed for a belly rub, Molly followed. Thirty minutes after arriving at our home, both girls were back to back on the bed while I rubbed Lu's belly with my right hand and Molly's with my left. Their heads arched back into each other, and together they made the shape of a heart.

Those moments were heartening, but Molly was still skittish. Sudden movements made her cringe, and anyone watching me try to clean out her ears would think I was killing her. She wouldn't approach either of us if we were looking at her, and she had a strong negative reaction to any attempt to touch her feet. She was terrified of any other dogs except Lulu, and even the sight of other dogs would make her bark like a maniac. We worried she would never be a well-socialized dog, and to top it all off, every time the door opened she attempted to escape.

Then we began to see small changes. More than snacks or walks, Molly loved affection. She came to trust us more and climb on our laps as we watched television. She became a bit demanding, even, shoving her nose under our hands when she thought we should be petting her instead of reading or folding clothes. She even started playing with toys and initiating games of "Chase me, I have the toy!" She and Lulu started "talking" back and forth in moans and wails that only my husband and I found endearing. But all of that came crashing to a halt when we started packing up the house to move to new jobs in Georgia.

Something in the proceedings triggered a setback, and our little girl seemed to be reliving a past trauma that shattered her trust in us. She became frantic when we left the house, and she would not eat. She began having accidents in the house, and the one time Lulu had to go to the vet and Molly was left home alone, Molly's wails of protest could be heard down the street.

The time to move finally came, and Lulu, Molly, and I drove the ten hours to Georgia to close on the new house. We stayed in a hotel while my husband followed two days later with the cat, iguana, and moving truck. Molly became increasingly anxious during the hotel stay, and even my husband's arrival didn't seem to soothe her. But when Lulu and Molly finally got to investigate their new home, Molly suddenly became her old self again. She staked out a sunny room, and that's where we put her kennel. Then she and Lulu took up guard positions near the big picture windows. Because our yard wasn't as big as the one in our former home, the first order of business after moving in was to find the off-leash dog park. The next Saturday we arrived at the park, and we hoped Molly would socialize. She barked at every dog who came in, but once the dog entered, she was ready to make friends. I was embarrassed by her behavior and worried that someone might think I had brought a dangerous animal to the park. Fortunately, everyone understood that Molly needed a little patience and tolerance, and she would learn. The goodhearted comment that she was "the welcome dog" made me relax and realize that others also saw that she just needed a chance.

Six months on, Molly has regained her ability to follow the basic commands we had worked on before the move. She also suddenly began fetching and following more complicated commands. Now Molly regularly plays with the dogs next door and happily welcomes dogs into the house to share toys and play games of chase. She has also trained me to play a game with her where I act like a monster and she hides in a favorite place, letting me "get" her (which involves loud noises, belly rubs, and many kisses).

Molly has a great capacity for games of pretend and a high emotional intelligence, which makes her a favorite among small children. We took her to the country where she could run off leash, and she showed us for the first time how incredibly fast she is. She has bonded to us so well that not only does she not let us out of her sight, but she returns on a dime. She even loves to have her ears cleaned out, and she will let anybody do anything to her feet. She's not perfect—she has eaten more iPod headphones than I care to think about—but our diminutive dog has lots of confidence and a big personality.

While at a "Dog Days" event recently, we received a magnet with dog on it that read, "I have to ask, am I adopted?" I jokingly asked my husband what we would say if Molly really asked us that. He looked at Molly and answered seriously, "You were always ours. We just had to find you."

 *Tamara Powell*

Shepherd Shorts

Heartworm? Negative. When he came into rescue from a life on the streets, Nugan was heartworm positive, which can be fatal even when treated. First, Nugan received an uncomfortable injection of worm killing medication, requiring him to stay at the vet for a week. When his foster mom came to pick him up, he was delirious with happiness to not have been left. After several weeks of leash-only walking and mostly crate confinement, Nugan began to feel better as the oxygen level in his blood increased with the death of the heartworms. This made Nugan want to be more active, but, alas, he had to remain calm for six weeks. At least he had a cat to keep him company. -*April Mitchem*

Learning and Loss

Did Sugar save me or did I save her? It was as much one as the other.

Almost 12 years ago I decided to adopt a German Shepherd. I wanted a large, tri-color male for companionship and protection, yet I ended up rescuing an abused, white female with enough phobias and insecurities to fill a psychology journal. It turns out we both had a lot to learn, and this is what she taught me:

- The best dogs in the world often start out as the worst.

- You can gain incredible self-worth by not giving up on a dog.

- Your dog may chew up your life, but material possessions aren't worth getting upset about.

- And most of all: If you give the gifts of companionship, love, and redemption, they will be returned to you tenfold (which has led me to become a foster for German Shepherd Dogs).

Sugar was a constant and assuring presence in my life for eleven years, and it's been impossible to think of living without her in it. But finally I have had to start doing just that, as she died in August from conditions related to arthritis. There will always be a big hole in my life without Sugar.

I kept this short because, as those of us who have lost a loved one know, words are never enough.

 *Debbie Tomblin*

About Happy Tails Books™

Happy Tails Books™ was created to help support animal rescue efforts by showcasing the love, happiness, and joy adopted dogs have to offer. With the help of animal rescue groups, stories are submitted by people who have adopted dogs, and then Happy Tails Books™ compiles them into breed-specific books. These books serve not only to entertain, but also to educate readers about dog adoption and the characteristics of each specific type of dog. Happy Tails Books™ donates a significant portion of proceeds back to the rescue groups who help gather stories for the books.

 **Happy Tails Books™** To submit a story or learn about other books Happy Tails Books™ publishes, please visit our website at http://happytailsbooks.com.

We're Writing Books About Your Favorite Dogs!

Schnauzer Chihuahua Golden Retriever PUG
DACHSHUND German Shepherd Collie Boxer
Labrador Retriever Husky Beagle ALL AMERICAN
Border Collie Pit Bull Terrier Shih Tzu Miniature Pinscher
Chow Chow Australian Shepherd Rottweiler Greyhound
Boston Terrier Jack Russell Poodle Cocker Spaniel
GREAT DANE Doberman Pinscher Yorkie SHEEPDOG
ST. BERNARD Pointer Blue Heeler

Find Them at Happytailsbooks.com!

Make your dog famous!

Do you have a great story about your adopted dog? We are looking for stories, poems, and even your dog's favorite recipes to include on our website and in upcoming books! Please visit the website below for story guidelines and submission instructions. **http://happytailsbooks.com/ submit.htm**